FOUNDATIONS
FOR OUR
FAITH

Volume 1

ADRIAN ROGERS

innovopublishing.com

Published by Innovo Publishing, LLC
www.innovopublishing.com
1-888-546-2111

Providing Full-Service Publishing Services for
Christian Authors, Artists & Ministries: Hardbacks, Paperbacks, eBooks,
Audiobooks, Music, Film & Courses

Foundations For Our Faith (Volume 1)

Unless otherwise noted, all scripture quoted is
from the King James Version (KJV) of the Bible.

ISBN: 978-1-61314-445-9

Cover Design & Interior Layout: Innovo Publishing, LLC
Printed in the United States of America
U.S. Printing History
First Edition: 1998
Second Edition: 2019

CONTENTS

ABOUT DR. ADRIAN ROGERS
AND
LOVE WORTH FINDING

K nown for his evangelistic zeal and uncompromising commitment to the Word of God, Adrian Rogers was one of the greatest preachers, respected Bible teachers, and Christian leaders of our time. For over fifty years, he consistently presented the Good News of Jesus Christ with strong conviction, compassion, and integrity.

Under his pastoral leadership, Bellevue Baptist Church in Memphis, Tennessee, grew from 9,000 members in 1972 to more than 29,000 at his retirement in 2005. And Adrian Rogers was a leader in his denomination, serving three terms as president of the Southern Baptist Convention.

In 1987, Adrian Rogers founded Love Worth Finding Ministries to broadcast and publish God's truth around the world through radio, television, print, and now online. Love Worth Finding can be heard in more than 150 countries, and continues to provide Adrian Rogers' messages around the clock.

These study guides are straight out of Adrian Rogers' messages and will provide hope, clarity, love, and truth as you study God's Word.

ABOUT THIS STUDY GUIDE

To help you delve deeper into God's Word and learn step-by-step how to apply His principles to your life, Love Worth Finding offers this study guide. It is ideal for family devotions, neighborhood Bible studies, or Sunday School, as well as for your own personal study. The guide is designed to be used in conjunction with Dr. Rogers' *Foundations For Our Faith* series available at LWF.org. To assist you in using the study guide, each lesson is broken down into sections:

Overview
The Overview gives a capsulated thought to set the scene for the lesson.

Introduction
The Introduction provides a concise snapshot of the passage being studied.

Discussion
The Discussion summarizes Dr. Rogers' teaching on the material covered in each lesson and provides a basis for continued study.

Application
The Application section contains questions designed to challenge the reader to look deeper into the biblical text and to find answers with practical application to life. This section is especially helpful when using the series for small group study.

Digging Deeper
Digging Deeper pulls together the message of the lesson and adds more insight, often elaborating on items of historical or cultural relevance.

INTRODUCTION

I n 1787, a Constitutional Convention was organized in Philadelphia, Pennsylvania. Twelve of the thirteen states sent 55 representatives to the meeting, a corporate body as profound as any ever assembled for the purpose of government. Men like George Washington, Benjamin Franklin, and James Madison led the Convention in writing the nation's most important document: the Constitution of the United States of America.

Since the Constitution was ratified in 1789, it has been amended, but never replaced. It has been attacked, but never defeated. It has been challenged, but never conquered. It has, for more than 200 years, served the purpose outlined in its profound 52-word Preamble. It has been a benchmark of principles, a bastion of liberty, and a bellwether of freedom for liberty lovers around the world.

The Christian faith has a document similar to the Constitution. It is called the book of Romans. Its 9,425 words (KJV) have for nearly 2,000 years been the doctrinal foundation for Christendom. Granted, the entire Bible serves that purpose in a larger way. All of its 66 books are the inspired, inerrant, and infallible words of God to mankind. But in a special way, the book of Romans serves as the theological cornerstone for the preeminent Good News that God has a plan for the redemption of sinners.

To the apostle Paul, the author of Romans, God entrusted the "mystery" of the Gospel. This mystery, while in seed form in the Old Testament, comes to fruition in Romans. There, the entire scope of God's Gospel—His Good News—is outlined: Man's sin is overcome and salvation is provided, leading to the sanctification of those who believe. God's sovereignty in salvation leads to the sacrifice of worship and service of the church—all to the glory of God.

You hold in your hands Volume I of a three-volume study guide to the book of Romans. While innumerable volumes have been penned by the great theological minds of the centuries, this offering has a distinct mission: to move theology off the library shelf and into the heart of the believer!

My goal is to offer you the same encouragement from Romans that I offer the precious flock I am privileged to shepherd as pastor. Theology is for life, and life is for living abundantly (John 10:10)! Therefore, the highly theological but eminently practical book of Romans is a book that every Christian should know intimately.

I trust you will know God's Good News from Romans better than ever before when you have finished studying this "Constitution of the Christian Faith."

THE BOOK THAT CHANGED THE WORLD

Overview

Though many important books have changed the world, none can equal the influence of the Bible. But within the library of Holy Scripture, perhaps no book reflects the heart of God and the passion of man as powerfully as the book of Romans.

Introduction: Romans 1:1

It is amazing how many times books have been the historical foundations of movements. Adolf Hitler's twisted mind produced *Mein Kampf* (My Battle), in which he espoused his Nazi philosophies. The ultimate results of his thoughts were a horrendous world war, gas ovens of the Holocaust, six million Jews exterminated, and thousands more lives ruined.

Hitler got many of his ideas from reading the books of the German philosopher Friedrich Nietzsche. This atheistic intellectual espoused the idea of the "superman," who is stronger than "man" and does not yield to traditional and cultural standards, but who overcomes them with the power of rational thinking and controlled passions. Nietzsche was a perverted atheist who declared blatantly, "God is dead!"

Another German, Karl Marx, wrote a three-volume work, *Das Kapital*, in which he promoted the idea of a classless society and the abolition of the capitalist form of economy. Written in the 1800s, his ideas were revived by the Russian revolutionary Vladimir Lenin in the early 20th century. The confluence of Marx's ideas and Lenin's leadership gave rise to the Russian revolution and the modern Communist movement. Untold millions of lives have been lost directly or indirectly as a result of Marxist-Leninist ideologies.

A British naturalist named Charles Darwin caused a scientific revolution with his books *The Origin of Species* (1859) and *The Descent of Man* (1871). He called into question the biblical teaching that man was the direct creation of God, and suggested that man evolved from lower life forms. The notion of biological evolution has devalued the biblical notion of human beings more than any other idea in history.

While these books have been powerful influences on mankind, no book has equaled the influence of the Bible. And within the Bible, we would be hard-pressed to say that any of the 66 books have been more influential in shaping Christendom, and the world, than the book of Romans.

Romans was the book that started the Protestant Reformation, when the Catholic monk Martin Luther discovered from Romans 1:17 that "the just shall live by faith." Augustine, one of the greatest theologians in church history, discovered salvation in Romans. John Wesley had his heart "strangely warmed", and later converted, after being introduced to the book of Romans. The English poet Coleridge said the book of Romans is the greatest piece of literature ever written.

Discussion

In this first lesson, we will spend our time developing an overview of the book, getting to know its author, and understanding its central themes.

The Contents of Romans

- Chapters 1-3 deal with the *sin* of mankind
- Chapters 4-6 deal with the *salvation* God provides for man.
- Chapters 7-8 deal with the process of *sanctification* of man—reversing the effects of sin.
- Chapters 9-11 deal with God's *sovereignty* in salvation.
- Chapter 12 deals with our *sacrifice* of ourselves to God in light of what He has done.
- Chapters 13-16 deal with our *service* to God, the evidence of our salvation.

You can see the logical progression of thought in this masterful book. The outline alone suggests how the contents might impact individuals, nations, even the world, in a lifechanging way.

The Author of Romans

Paul the apostle not only authored Romans, but is also the author of more New Testament books than any other writer. As was the custom in his day, he clearly identified himself in the opening lines of his letters: "Paul, a servant of Jesus Christ, called to be an apostle, separated Onto the gospel of God" (Romans 1:1).

Before we look at Paul's life in detail, let's take a quick glance at his biography. Paul, or "Saul" as he was known before his conversion to Christ, was a Jew, but a Jew who was also a Roman citizen. He was born in the Roman city of Tarsus, in modern Turkey, near the Mediterranean Sea. His stature as a

Roman citizen gave him rights not enjoyed by other Jews of the day. He could travel freely and did not experience the oppression and subjugation which the Jews in Israel did. He was also highly educated, spoke several languages, and was a student of the most famous Jewish teacher of the day, Gamaliel. His devotion to the Law of the Old Testament was widely known. He was a descendant of the tribe of Benjamin, had been circumcised on the eighth day in accordance with the Law, was a Pharisee, and was, in his own words, a "Hebrew of the Hebrews" (Philippians 3:5).

In other words, Paul was a rising young star in Israel, zealous to promote adherence to the Old Testament. But then this rising young star of Judaism came crashing to the earth. He had an experience which changed his life—and ours, as he yielded himself to God and became a mighty messenger of His Truth!

Paul Was Saved

Being saved by Christ on the Damascus road was a life-changing, name-changing, and world-changing experience for Paul. Before he met Christ on the Damascus road, Paul's name was Saul. King Saul in the Old Testament was a man of stature, both physically and in ego. In fact, it is his brazen ego that ultimately cost him his kingship. When Christ confronted Saul on the road to Damascus (where Saul was going to persecute Christians; see Acts 9), He said, "Saul, Saul, why persecutest thou me?" (Acts 9:4). The great Saul of Tarsus, not unlike Saul of the Old Testament, found himself cut down to size by God. He went from being Saul, the Hebrew of the Hebrews, to Paul, "the least of all saints" (Ephesians 3:8), And becoming an apostle didn't change his view of himself either, because he later said that he was "the least of the apostles" (1 Corinthians 15:9).

Knowing he was a nobody didn't give him an inferiority complex. Rather, it gave him a correct view of humanity and the grace of God. Later, in reading the book of Romans, we see the depth of Paul's understanding of the grace that saved him.

Paul Was Surrendered

Romans 1:1 tells us that, besides being saved, Paul was a servant to Jesus Christ. This man, who had more learning than most in Israel, surrendered to and became the servant of the son of a carpenter from Nazareth. Paul uses the Greek word *doulos* to describe his status as a surrendered bond-servant.

The Law in Israel stipulated that every seven years, those who had become enslaved to pay off their debt were to be set free. But if the slave chose to, he could remain the property of his master. If he had been well cared for and had a secure place in the household, he could choose to remain a slave. But he would become a bond-slave of the master. He would have a small hole punched in his earlobe, and the scar would signify his lifelong commitment as a bond-slave. Paul, therefore, was a bond-slave of the Lord Jesus Christ. He willingly submitted himself to Jesus as his master.

Paul Was Sent

The next thing we learn about Paul from Romans 1:1 fits exactly with his status of being a bond-servant of Christ—that he was called. Christ, the master, called Paul, the bond-servant, to be an apostle. Literally, "apostle" means "a sent one." Paul didn't get saved and then start looking around for a Christian vocation, deciding apostleship looked pretty interesting. No, Christ called Paul to be an apostle, and he obeyed.

May I tell you something else about being called by Christ? Christ does not call just apostles—or just pastors, or evangelists, or church leaders. He calls each believer to Himself. Romans 1:6 calls the members of the church in Rome, to whom Paul is writing this letter, "the called of Jesus Christ." That means you and I have a calling from Christ just as unique as Paul's calling.

His call reflects His love for each member of His body individually. Paul was called as an apostle, and you and I are called as well. It is my calling as a pastor that keeps me confident that He is going to use me. And you should have that same confidence about your calling. Paul's example as an obedient bond-servant who responded to the Master's call is an example for us to follow, just as he said: "Be ye followers of me, even as I also am of Christ" (1 Corinthians 11:1).

Paul Was Separated

Paul was also separated: "separated unto the gospel of God" (Romans 1:1). The key word in this description of Paul is not "separated," it is what he was separated unto: the Gospel of God. Paul had been a separated man all of his life. He had been separated (meaning "set apart") unto a life of strict adherence to the Mosaic laws of Judaism. Paul didn't just leave Judaism, or the strict adherence to the law, He moved toward something else—the Gospel. It does no good to stop doing the wrong thing if you don't start doing the right thing. If you separate yourself from, but don't then separate yourself unto, you have done only half of what you should.

The word "separated" is the Greek word from which we get our word "horizon." If you stand on a tall building and survey the horizon, it looks a certain way. But if you change your location, go up in a different building in a different city, the horizon looks different. Therefore, what determines your horizon is your location, your center. From where you stand, your horizon forms the boundary of your world. You are set apart unto that world that is defined by your horizon.

Becoming a Christian is like moving to a new location and viewing a new horizon. Your center changes. Your center becomes Christ, and His life becomes the boundary of your life. That's what it means to be separated unto Christ and His Gospel.

The Hero of Romans

In Romans 1:3 Paul tells us who the hero of his story is. His letter concerns God's Son, "Jesus Christ our Lord." Let's look now at four ways that Paul describes Jesus Christ who is the focus of Romans.

Christ Is the Promised One

God's Gospel was "promised afore by his prophets in the holy Scriptures" (Romans 1:2). It's amazing that the foundation of everything Paul is going to tell us about sin, salvation, sanctification, sovereignty, sacrifice, and service has its foundation in the "holy Scriptures"—the Old Testament that Paul had been studying all his life! Jesus is not only the hero of Romans, He is also the prophesied hero of the Old Testament. Jesus told the Jews to "Search the scriptures; for in them ye think ye have eternal life: and they are they which testify of me" (John 5:39).

Christ Is the Provided One

But not only is He the promised one, He is the provided one. What do I mean by this? I mean exactly what Paul says in Romans 1:3-4, that God provided exactly what the human race needed in providing Jesus Christ. He was fully human ("the seed of David according to the flesh"), and He was fully divine ("declared to be the Son of God with power ... by the resurrection from the dead"). He was the God-Man, perfect humanity and perfect deity united in one person. Only God could save mankind, and only man could die in the place of mankind. Jesus Christ was provided by God to be both.

Christ Is the Powerful One

Verse 4 of Romans 1 holds the key to how we know that Christ was not just a wild-eyed fanatic, a guru, or a religious teacher—He was resurrected from the dead! By conquering death, hell, sin, and the grave, Jesus demonstrated that the One who had called Paul to be an apostle was a Powerful One. And because of His power, He can deal with our sin, provide for our salvation and sanctification, and be sovereign over the affairs of our lives.

Christ Is the Pure One

Jesus' power was anointed by "the Spirit of holiness" (Romans 1:4). As the writer of the Epistle to the Hebrews says,

Jesus was "holy, harmless, undefiled, separate from sinners" (Hebrews 7:26). His purity and holiness gave credibility and authority to His message. Paul never found Jesus to be less than a holy Savior.

The Theme of Romans

If Romans has Jesus Christ as its hero, what is its theme? If we suspected that it had something to do with the hero's purpose in life, we would be right! The theme of the book of Romans is the Gospel. The mission of the hero of Romans was to redeem mankind from sin, and the Gospel is the Good News that He succeeded in His mission. Romans becomes the fullest explanation in Scripture, and in the world, of God's Good News—the Gospel—that redemption has been accomplished.

We conclude this first lesson on Romans by identifying what Paul says about the Gospel: its source, its subject, and its supply.

The Source of the Gospel

The reason Paul never wavered in his understanding of the Gospel is because he knew its source was God. It was not to be changed. He warned the Galatians, "If any man preach any other gospel unto you than that ye have received, let him be accursed" (Galatians 1:9). Paul knew that a false gospel could lead only to a false salvation. God's salvation can be received only if the Gospel is clear.

The Subject of the Gospel

If the Gospel is God's, what is His intent? It is "concerning his Son Jesus Christ" (Romans 1:3). It is about the birth, life, death, and resurrection of Jesus Christ—no one else! The reason we have so many moral worldlings in our churches is because they haven't met the Subject of the Gospel. They haven't met Jesus. They've met the church, the denomination, the pastor, the choir, the Sunday School teacher—but they haven't met Jesus. Christianity is not a creed, a code, or a cause—it is Christ. Take Him out of the Gospel, and you no longer have Christianity.

The Supply of the Gospel

The source and supply of the Gospel of God, concerning Jesus Christ, is the grace of God (Romans 1:5). Grace is the gift of God that saves people like us apart from our works. It is the sheer, absolute free gift of God. That's what exploded in the mind of Martin Luther: The just shall live by faith! We are not saved by good works, by religion, by baptism, by church membership, by giving money. We are saved by the grace of God.

No other book of the Bible is as full of the grace of God as the book of Romans. My prayer is that, as you study this book, you will come to understand why Romans has been called "The Constitution of Christianity." But more importantly, it is my prayer that the Gospel of the grace of God will become your own personal possession.

Application

1. Read Philippians 3:4-6. List all the reasons Paul had to think highly of himself before his conversion to Christ:

   Circumcised the 8th day, of state of Israel, from tribe of Benjamin a hebrew of Hebrews + a Pharisee

   Read Acts 22:3-5. Add any additional insights about Paul's stature as a Jew before meeting Christ: 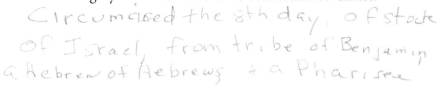 a Jew, born in Tarsus, city of Cilicia taught by Gamaliel. zealous toward God. persecuted Christians

Now read 2 Corinthians 11:21-28. List the things that Paul had to boast about after becoming a Christian.

a minister of Christ, bold in the Lord, a Hebrew was beaten, stoned, in prison etc. the care of the churches

What other things could he have taken pride in after becoming a Christian (2 Corinthians 12:12)?

did signs, wonders, & mighty deeds he was an apostle

Based on the above passages, describe the change in Paul's life and priorities. *was an apostle not a pharisee, concerned about serving Christ not the law.*

What seemed to be most important to Paul after becoming a Christian (2 Corinthians 12:9-10)?

the power of God to rest upon him.

List any significant changes in your priorities, and goals that occurred when you became a Christian.

Centered on Christ, I am prayer intercessor

2. Was Paul's life easier or harder after becoming a bondservant of Christ?

harder

Why do you think Paul was willing to remain a bondservant of Jesus Christ?

Because he knew he was called by God to serve Christ & preach salvation to the Gentiles

You are not forced against your will to remain a Christian. Why do you? What is it about having Jesus Christ as a Master that causes you to remain His bond-servant?

Jesus is my life, and I want to please him

3. How did you enter into the grace of God (Galatians 1:6)?

God calls us into his Grace

Once called, what is your responsibility as a Christian (Ephesians 4:1)? *You walk/ worthy of the vocation you are called.*

What kind of calling have you received (Philippians 3:14; Thessalonians 4:7; 2 Timothy 1:9)? *Intercessor, called us to holiness, called to holiness according to God's purpose + grace.*

As Paul was called to be an apostle, to what area of service do you feel you are called as a Christian?

Intercession

4. When was Paul separated unto the Gospel (Galatians 1:15)?

   from our mother's womb

   When was Jeremiah set apart as a prophet for God
   (Jeremiah 1:5)?

   In his mother's womb

   How about David? When did God begin to shape his life
   (Psalm 139:13-16)?

   In his mother's womb

   What evidence is there in your life that you are "set apart"
   for the purposes of God?

   my passion for Christ

5. In what ways in your life has Jesus Christ shown Himself to be "the Powerful One"? *my prayers are answered.*

6. Write out in your words a definition of "the Gospel of Jesus Christ." *Jesus died for our sins in our place by his blood. He paid the death penalty so we could have eternal life.*

What is "the Gospel" according to I Corinthians 15:1-4?

Jesus died for our sins he was buried, and rose again the third day.

Digging Deeper

As a Christian, you have been called by God. Take out a sheet of paper and write at the top, "Why I Am Thankful God Called Me to Himself." Then, start writing! Make a list of all the reasons you are thankful God called you and set you apart to be close to Him. Be practical, and be honest. Think of God's faithfulness, and how life would be different today if He had not called you to know Him. When you have finished, keep your list in your Bible. Take one item each day and give thanks to God for it in prayer.

LESSON
2

TOTALLY ABANDONED TO THE GOSPEL

Overview

That which comes out of our mouth in time defines who we are. The apostle Paul made three "I am" statements which reveal clearly who he is. Can you echo his words in your, own life?

Introduction: Romans 1:14-10

In this lesson we'll study the heart and mind of a man who was totally abandoned to the Gospel of Jesus Christ. If you will look at a man and get beneath the surface, get down into his heart, understand his motivation, see the philosophy of his life—then you'll be able to understand him. In my estimation the apostle Paul is the greatest Christian who ever lived, and I believe we get a glimpse of Paul's true heart in Romans 1:14-16:

> *I am debtor both to the Greeks, and to the Barbarians; both to the wise, and to the unwise. So, as much as*

*in me is, I am ready to preach the gospel to you that
are at Rome also. For I am not ashamed of the gospel
of Christ: for it is the power of God unto salvation to
every one that believeth; to the Jew first, and also to
the Greek.*

There are three "I am" statements in this passage. In verse
14 he says, "I am debtor." Look in verse 15 and underscore, "I am
ready." Then look in verse 16: "I am not ashamed." Now if you
put those three "I am's" together, you're going to understand what
motivated the greatest pioneer and spokesman of the church who
ever lived. He preached and was a missionary just a few short
years after Jesus Christ ascended to heaven. Amazingly, when
Paul himself went to heaven, there was a Christian church, a little
colony of heaven, in every major city in the Roman Empire.

A little man who had a heart aflame for Almighty God said,
I am debtor ... I am ready ... I am not ashamed." How important
it is that each believer in Christ agree with the apostle Paul, and
be able to say those same three things. Paul certainly wanted
every believer to be like him in that regard, and rightfully so.
Remember that he said, "Be ye followers of me, even as I also
am of Christ" (1 Corinthians 11:1). Paul does not say this out of
ego or pride. He says this because he is acting out the answers
to very important questions he asked the Lord Jesus at the time
of his conversion—"Who art thou, Lord?" and "Lord, what wilt
thou have me to do?" (Acts 9:5, 6). What you see lived out in the
life of the apostle Paul are Jesus' answers to those two questions.

In this lesson, we will look beneath the surface of Paul's life
and see what our lives will look like if we imitate him. We will
discover that if we imitate Paul, we will be a debtor, we will be
ready, and we will not be ashamed of the Gospel of Jesus Christ.

Discussion

Who are you? Who am I? The "I am" statements we make
about ourselves paint a picture of who we are. We can describe
ourselves as tall or short, young or old, thin or ... well, you get
the idea. But those are just surface descriptions that describe us

physically. What we are in the inner man, the person of the heart, is really what God is concerned with and what should be most important to us (1 Samuel 16:7). Paul's own words paint a picture of who he is in the most critical area of life—his relationship to his Savior's Gospel.

Paul Was Faithful to the Obligations of the Gospel ("I Am Debtor...")

First of all, Paul says, "I am debtor." That tells me that Paul was faithfull to the obligations of the Gospel. Remember in Romans 1:1 Paul calls himself a servant? He was literally a bond-servant—someone who had been purchased and then who wanted to serve his master willingly and voluntarily. Paul wrote to the Corinthians, Ye are bought with a price; be not ye the servants of men" (1 Corinthians 7:23). There is no question that Paul saw himself as a debtor. But a debtor to whom?

Debtor to the Lord Jesus Christ

First of all, Paul saw himself as a debtor to the Lord Jesus Christ. Do you? Do you see yourself in debt to Jesus or do you say, "I thought salvation was free"? It is free to us, but don't we sing these words also, "Jesus paid it all and all to him I owe"? Nothing in life is free, including our eternal salvation. Jesus Christ paid for our salvation and gave it to us as a gift. And I am a debtor to the one who hung in agony and blood on that cross for me. He paid for my life with His life. If we imitate the apostle Paul, we will see ourselves as a debtor to Christ.

Debtor to the Heroes of the Past

Along with the apostle Paul, we are debtors to the heroes of the past. For instance, Paul was a debtor to Stephen who was martyred for his faith which Paul witnessed. Paul was a debtor to the Old Testament prophets who preached the word faithfully in Israel down through the centuries, and who recorded the truth so that Paul could study it under Gamaliel. There are many heroes of the faith—the great cloud of witnesses mentioned in Hebrews 12:1—to whom we are debtors.

There are many who have lived in our day to whom we are indebted, as well. Who paid for the nice, warm, beautiful church building you sit in each Sunday? Who taught your Sunday School lessons when you were a child? Many have sacrificed that we might enjoy an abundant spiritual life. We are debtors to them all.

Debtor to Those Around Us

Finally, we are debtor to all of those around us. Notice what Paul says in verse 14: "I am debtor both to the Greeks, and to the Barbarians; both to the wise, and to the unwise." When he says the Greeks and the Barbarians, he's talking about the cultured and the non-cultured, the "up and out" and the "down and out," the educated and the ignorant, the rich and the poor. He's saying everybody needs to know Jesus who said, "freely ye have received, freely give" (Matthew 10:8).

Here's what it means to be a debtor to those around us. Suppose you were charged by the governor of the state to deliver a pardon to a man on death row in the state prison. You get distracted with your own business and forget all about the man until you read about his execution in the paper. Then it hits you— you had the document that would save his life but failed to deliver it on time!

My friend, you and I have the Gospel message that will save every person sentenced to eternal death. And we are under a debt—an obligation—to deliver that message. But will we? Or will we get so distracted with our own affairs that we fail to "pay our debt" to those around us? Paul did not fail those who were around him, and if we imitate him, neither will we.

Paul Was Flexible For Opportunities For The Gospel ("I Am Ready. . .")

The second "I am" that Paul spoke about indicates flexibility in the spread of the Gospel. He says in verse 15, "So, as much as in me is, I am ready to preach the gospel to you that are at Rome also." Not only was Paul faithful where he was, he was flexible to go wherever the Lord would send him. And Rome seemed to be high on his itinerary.

Why was Paul able to be so flexible, to go wherever the Lord sent him? Because he was not afraid to die. He had no fear of his next assignment. For Paul, "to live is Christ, and to die is gain" (Philippians 1:21). Paul was a great witness for Christ because he himself was part of the evidence. Jesus died and Paul was ready to die. Paul was just like Jesus in so many regards.

We know from Scripture that Paul was incarcerated on more than one occasion. In fact, we believe that he was martyred for his faith in the city of Rome. I have stood in the prison cell in Rome where Paul was reportedly kept prior to his death, and I can just imagine the shock on the face of the Roman guards the day he was killed. They looked into the face of a man who was not worried about death. Why? Because Paul would say to his executioners, "I die daily" (1 Corinthians 15:31).

Are you and I that flexible? Are we as flexible as the apostle Paul, or the great missionary David Livingstone? It was he who prayed, "Send me where you will but go with me. Lay any burden on my heart but sustain me. Sever any tie but the one that binds my heart to thee." The apostle Paul was flexible. David Livingstone was flexible. Are you and I flexible as well?

Paul Was Fearless Towards Opposition To The Gospel ("I Am Not Ashamed. . .")

Are you getting a glimpse of the kind of person the apostle Paul was? This third "I am" will complete the picture: "For I am not ashamed of the gospel of Christ: for it is the power of God unto salvation to every one that believeth; to the Jew first, and also to the Greek" (verse 16). There were many reasons in Paul's day why a weak person might have been ashamed of the Gospel. The person, purpose, power, and plan of the Gospel message were all subject to the ridicule of the world. They were then, and they are today. That's why we need to learn from Paul.

Not Ashamed of the Person of the Gospel

In the first place, the Gospel of Jesus Christ was identified with a poor, Jewish carpenter who was crucified. Can you imagine going to Rome, the Imperial City, with its might, power, and armies, and saying, "I want to tell you about the son of a Jewish carpenter who died for your sins"?

Rome had no appreciation for the Jews. Why, hadn't Rome subjugated the land of Judea? Why should Rome listen to anything that would come out of a conquered place? And if Rome had no appreciation for Jews, how much less would they have for a Christian, which they considered just an irritating religious sect? Christians were the scum of the earth in that day. Even Paul himself, when he went to Rome, went as a prisoner. But Paul was bold for the Lord Jesus anyway. He was fearless and not ashamed.

Now, I want to ask you a question: Are you ashamed of the Gospel? Are you ashamed to put a Bible on your desk at work? Are you ashamed to bow your head in prayer in the cafeteria? Are you ashamed to invite people to know Jesus Christ? Are you ashamed of the One who died for you? You shouldn't be. Think of the sixty billion or so people who have lived on this earth during recorded history. You follow the One who has had the greatest impact of them all.

The name of Jesus is above the names of all the scientists; philosophers, doctors, inventors, and pioneers. None have done what He has done. If Paul was not ashamed of Him in the first few years of the expansion of the Gospel, why should we be after 2,000 years of seeing the good He has done?

Not Ashamed of the Purpose of the Gospel

Not only was Paul not ashamed of the person of the Gospel, he was not ashamed of the purpose of the Gospel—the salvation of souls. He says in verse 16, "I am not ashamed of the gospel of Christ:"—that's the person of the Gospel—"for it is the power of God unto salvation to every one that believth"—that's the purpose of the Gospel.

One day I was listening to a political talk show and reading some of the newspapers. I thought to myself, "How vain, how silly. They're trying everything they can to save civilization." The Gospel is not intended to save civilization from wreckage, but to save people from the wreckage of civilization. Jesus came not as a social engineer, but as the Savior of mankind, Luke 19:10 says, "For the Son of man is come to seek and to save that which was lost."

There are many kinds of losses in fife. It's tragic to lose your health, wealth, friends, loved ones, or your life. But how much more tragic it would be to lose your soul! "For what shall it profit a man, if he shall gain the whole world, and lose his own soul?" (Mark 8:36). How could we be ashamed of the Gospel when the Gospel is the only thing that can help this world today? The Gospel is the only thing that can make harlots pure, drunkards sober, perverts straight, and adulterers pure. The Gospel is the only thing that can give hope that is steadfast and true. It is the lifeline to rescue the perishing and care for the dying and snatch them in pity from sin and the grave. That's the purpose of the Gospel!

Not Ashamed of the Power of the Gospel

Any purpose will fall flat if it has no power. Paul knew that the Gospel "is the power of God unto salvation" (verse 16). The word that he uses for power is the Greek word from which we get our English words *dynamite, dynamo,* and *dynamic.* This world is enamored with power. 'We've heard so much in our generation about atomic power. But if you were to take an atomic bomb and detonate it between the lapels of your coat, there wouldn't be enough of you to bury. You'd be vaporized! But that wouldn't take the sin out of your heart.

There's only one power that can wash and make you whiter than snow. That is the incredible power of the Gospel. When you receive Christ, you become His vessel of dynamic power! I've been living for Jesus since my teenage years and I can attest that, were it not for the power of the Gospel in my heart, I would not have persevered to this point.

Not Ashamed of the Plan of the Gospel

Finally, Paul is not ashamed of the plan of the Gospel. Here it is: "to every one that believeth" (verse 16). Aren't you glad there are no conditions on being saved? We don't have to read the Bible, get baptized, give a hundred dollars—we just choose to believe. God's simple, wonderful, glorious plan is that anybody, anywhere, anytime can say, "Lord Jesus, come into my heart and save me." And He will! Paul was not ashamed to offer a Gospel whose plan included only one requirement. He didn't care if it made him look simple or unsophisticated. He wasn't building a religion with a set of rules. He was offering a relationship with a Savior—the Savior of whom he was not ashamed.

If you can answer, "I am..." along with Paul, then the world will know who you are, and soon will know who Jesus is as well.

Application

1. Who are you? In the spirit of Paul's confession ("I am..."), and without fear of being boastful, write down at least five honest statements that describe who you are in your spiritual life.

   a. I am ... more than a conquerer

   b. I am ... redeemed

   c. I am ... justified

   d. I am ... sanctified

   e. I am ... crucified with Christ

Now, write down at least three more "I am" statements that describe who you would like to become spiritually in the future.

a. I am ... _not afraid_

b. I am ... _kind_

c. I am ... _humble_

2. Read Romans 1:14. Who are the people who blazed the spiritual trail that you followed to Christ, or who have helped you grow in Christ? _IM Derek Prince, J Farag_

How could you tangibly express your gratitude toward them?

Who are the Greeks and Barbarians (verse 14; those who haven't received the Gospel) that you live or work with each day, to whom you are a debtor? _my neighbors unsaved loved ones,_

If you were to imitate the apostle Paul, what would you do about your relationship to these people? *Witness to them*

3. Read Acts 16:6-10. What do you learn about Paul's flexibility from this passage? *he changed his plans and did what the Holy spirit told him, to do*

What plan of Paul's was thwarted in verse 6?

they didn't preach in Asia,

What plan was stopped in verse 7?

they didn't go to Bithynia,

Who was changing Paul's plans? *the Holy Spirit was changing his plans*

What evidence do you find that Paul was upset or distraught over these changes? *He obeyed immediately*

Instead of Paul's original plans, what plan does God lay before them in verse 9? *they went to Macedonia Instead*

What key word do you find in verse 10 that indicates how promptly Paul responded to the Lord's leading? *he went immediately.*

How does this key word figure into your own response to the Lord or your own flexibility in the things of the Gospel? *to go and not delay.*

4. Read the following verses and record what you learn about not being ashamed of the Gospel:

- Romans 9:33 _we should not be ashamed_
- Romans 10:11 _we should not be ashamed of the gospel_

[Note: it is helpful to remember that the following verses in Philippians and 2 Timothy were written while Paul was in prison for the sake of the Gospel.]

- Philippians 1:20

- 2 Timothy 1:8

- 2 Timothy 1:12

- 2 Timothy 1:16

- 2 Timothy 2:15

Digging Deeper

Read Exodus 3:14-15 and John 8:58-59. What was God the Father saying about Himself in Exodus? What was Jesus saying when He applied God's name to Himself in the Gospel of John? The name of God in Exodus 3 was so revered by Jews that they would not even pronounce it. The name "I am" was such an intimate form of self-disclosure that it was blasphemous to speak it. Paul didn't hesitate to define himself ("I am") in relation to Jesus, but never in promoting himself. How had the church in Corinth begun misusing the "I am" with reference to their human leaders? What did Paul do to correct them? (See 1 Corinthians 1:10-17).

LESSON
3

THE LOST WORLD

Overview

Question: What is the most terrible thing God could do to a culture? Answer: Nothing. Paul reveals that when God takes His hands off, His worst judgments are not far behind.

Introduction: Romans 1:18-31

The book of Romans has been called the Magna Carta of our faith, the Constitution of Christianity. It's the greatest theological treatise ever written, and with it in our hands and Christ in our heart, we can face whatever fife brings. Unfortunately, I believe that the future is bringing disaster and judgment our way.

One only need look at the lows we have attained in entertainment, the senselessness of crimes that are committed, the spread of sexually transmitted diseases, or the continual attacks on the unborn to know that America is on perilous ground. If you talk to some people and say that the problem is sin, they will disagree because today "sin" is a politically incorrect term. Do you know what the only sin is today? To call sin a sin. If you call sin a sin, many will say you are intolerant. A man may be sick but he's not sinful. He may be weak but he's not wicked. He may be ill but he's not evil. Even if you tell people that what they're doing is wrong, they offer an excuse. The environment, genetics, ignorance, upbringing—nobody wants to be blamed or accept responsibility for what they have done. This type of attitudinal shift will inevitably bring a response from God.

We're going to learn something in this lesson about the wrath and judgment of God. Before Paul gets around to the details of the Good News, he paints a very detailed picture of the bad news. It's the bad news that makes the good news good!

When my wife and I recently were told in an airport that our plane was going to leave on time, we began rejoicing excitedly. Do we do this every time a plane leaves on time? No, we do not. Shortly before we had been told that our plane's departure was going to be delayed by several hours. Therefore, it was the bad news that made the good news so good! And that's how it is with the Good News of the Gospel.

The average person doesn't know that "the wrath of God is revealed" against sin (Romans 1:18). But it is. It has been in the past, will be in the future, and is currently being revealed against sin. The wrath of God is not a hot topic. But the love of God (about which we hear a great deal) is never as powerfully received as it is when the wrath of God has been comparatively revealed. And why does Paul go into detail about the wrath of God? He tells us in the last six words of Romans 1:18-20:

> For the wrath of God is revealed from heaven against all ungodliness and unrighteousness of men, who hold the truth in unrighteousness; because that which may be known of God is manifest in them; for God hath showed it unto them. For the invisible things of him from the creation of the world are clearly seen, being understood by the things that are made, even his eternal power and Godhead; so that they are without excuse.

The one thing God will not accept as a response to sin is an excuse. A confession? Yes, but not an excuse. Before Paul presents the Gospel to every person, he demonstrates that every person stands in need of the Gospel—without excuse.

Discussion

Paul follows three lines of reasoning in Romans 1:18-31 to demonstrate why no person is without sin and why no person has an excuse for not honoring God in their life: willful self-determination, wicked self-deception, and woeful self-destruction.

Man's Willful Self-Determination

Even though God's existence, power, and authority are clearly revealed, man willfully determines to go his own way. The two things man must ignore in order to exercise his own self will are an inner witness (conscience) and an outer witness (creation).

Conscience

The witness of the truth about God, which every person already possesses, is the conscience: "that which may be known of God is manifest in them; for God hath showed it unto them" (Romans 1:19). There is a God-shaped vacuum in every man's heart. The Bible says that Christ is the light "which lighteth every man that cometh into the. world" (John 1:9). When a man says that he is an atheist, he is lying. He doesn't know he's lying, but deep down in his subconscious he has witness of the existence of God.

A man who owns an interstate trucking firm gave his new employees a lie-detector test. One of the questions was, "Do you believe in God?" Every time a person answered "No" the lie detector said he was telling a lie. Everybody comes into this world with a "God-consciousness." Whether they admit or recognize it is another question.

Creation

Not only is there the inner witness called conscience, but there is also the outer witness called creation. The evidence of God's presence is everywhere.

THE REVELATION OF GOD'S TRUTH

Look in verse 20: "For the invisible things of him from the creation of the world are clearly seen, being understood by the things that are made, even his eternal power and Godhead." What does that mean? It means if you have things that are made, you have to have a maker. If you have creation, it follows that there is a creator. You don't have to have a Ph.D. to figure that out. The atheist believes that nothing times nobody equals everything. Everything just happened. But the Bible says how it happened is clearly seen: God created it all. That's the reason the Psalmist said in Psalm 19 verses 1 through 4: "The heavens declare the glory of God; and the firmament showeth his handiwork."

THE REACH OF GOD'S TRUTH

The evidence of God's existence extends to all parts of His creation. Design and designer show that there is a God. Life is far too complicated, if examined in all its fullness, to truly believe that it just happened. This strains reasonableness, not to mention evidence. The evidence of God's creative presence is found in the smallest and the largest parts of the universe.

THE RESISTANCE TO GOD'S TRUTH

In spite of revelation and reach, there is resistance to God's truth and His presence. And that, in fact, becomes evidence of His presence. Have you ever tried to resist a force that doesn't exist? No one goes around leaning against the wind on a still day. But if you look out your window and see people struggling to walk straight, you know a powerful wind is blowing.

Look at verse 18: "For the wrath of God is revealed from heaven against all ungodliness and unrighteousness of men who hold the truth in unrighteousness." "Hold" is actually better translated "hold down" or "suppress." When you see people resisting the truth, there's evidence that the truth exists. I get letters from people who resist the truth they've heard me preach. It just confirms Romans 1:18 when their letters arrive.

Besides willful self-determination, there is another way that mankind tries to avoid the truth.

Man's Wicked Self-Deception

If a man denies the truth, he will believe something else. He will deceive himself into believing a lie. But why would man do that? There are three reasons, all of them related to the pride and ego of mankind. Sinful man would rather believe a lie of his own making than the truth of God's making.

Selfish Indifference

Verse 21 reveals man's selfish indifference: "Because that, when they knew God, they glorified him not as God, neither were thankful; but became vain in their imaginations, and their foolish heart was darkened." Anything to which you are indifferent will gradually shrink into oblivion. Truth denied gradually recedes into darkness. Every bit of light that is refused only increases the darkness. Many people selfishly are pursuing their own agendas and are indifferent to God's agenda. They don't realize that their indifference has the same effect as open resistance: the darkness increases where light is not received.

Sophisticated Ignorance

Verse 22 reveals the next problem: "Professing themselves to be wise, they became fools." There are so many who have the idea that they are too intelligent to believe in God. They have an air of sophistication about them and they refuse God's light. They think that if the best we know about God comes from a book written by a bunch of primitive people several thousand years ago—well, surely we have advanced beyond that. Surely we know now more than they did then.

Shameful Idolatry

Finally, shameful idolatry sets in. Some people resist the truth because of indifference, and some because of sophistication. But whatever the reason, if man doesn't worship the true God, he will eventually worship a false one: "And changed [the word literally means exchanged] the glory of the incorruptible God into an image made like to corruptible man, and to birds, and four-footed beasts, and creeping things" (verse 23). Man stops worshiping the incorruptible God and begins worshiping creeping things.

While it seems impossible to believe that man would go so low as to begin worshiping animals and insects, it has and does happen. Go to the museums in Cairo and you will see the scarabs, or sacred beetles, that were once worshiped by the Egyptians. Go to India today and you will see cows being worshiped. Even when man isn't 'worshiping the animal kingdom, he pursues another form of idolatry just as vile: he worships images of his own sinfulness.

An idol is only a magnified sinner. Man takes his worst vices—greed, lust, drunkenness, violence—and deifies them. He legitimatizes them when he deifies them. For example, you can go to Lebanon and see the mighty temple to the ancient god Bacchus, the god of drunkenness, whom the ancients worshiped by getting drunk. Or you can go to Corinth and see the temples where men worshiped the love goddess by having sex with temple prostitutes.

First, man manifests selfish indifference, then sophisticated ignorance, then shameful idolatry. He exchanges the truth for a lie and begins to worship the creation instead of the Creator.

What is the practical result of idolatry? Let's cite two seemingly unconnected events, and then show how Scripture ties them together. In 1962, God was removed from American public schools on the argumentative basis of separation of church and state. The generation who spent their school years in a spiritual vacuum has led the way in murdering millions of babies in their mothers' wombs. Remember: if you remove the light, the darkness of idolatry will come in.

This happened to Israel in the Old Testament as recorded in Psalm 106. God told them to destroy the idolatrous nations that could lead them astray, but they didn't (verse 34). They began to mingle with the heathen and "learned their works" (verse 35), and worshiped their idols, which became a snare to them (verse 36). Then they even began to sacrifice their children—the sons and daughters of Israel—"unto devils" (verse 37). They sacrificed their own children upon the altars of the idols of Canaan, and "the land was polluted with blood" (verse 38).

Does this sound familiar? Are American women—even some Christian women, with the approval of their husbands—killing their innocent children because they have bought into an idolatrous lie, "My body, my choice"? As a result, we can expect the same response from God toward us that He had toward Israel: "therefore was the wrath of the

Lord kindled against his people" (verse 40).

When man is indifferent to truth, and allows himself to be deceived, it is only a matter of time until he is destroyed. And the language of Romans tells us that God allows the destruction to be self-inflicted.

Man's Woeful Self-Destruction

There are three stages to man's self-destruction which are clearly laid out in Romans 1.

Stage One: Sexual Perversion

Paul says in Romans 1:26-27 that, following their idolatry,

> God gave them up unto vile affections: for even their women did change the natural use into that which is against nature: and likewise also the men, leaving the natural use of the woman, burned in their lust one toward another; men with men working that which is unseemly, and receiving in themselves that recompense of their error which was meet.

Paul is clearly talking about the sin of sodomy, or homosexuality. He calls it unclean, lustful, dishonorable, vile, and a sin against nature. There is no way that what is currently being touted as sexually acceptable in our society can incur anything but God's wrath.

The Scriptures are abundantly clear that sexual perversion is sin in God's sight. In the days of Lot, in which homosexuality was rampant, sexual perversion brought about the destruction of Sodom (Luke 17:28-30). Peter confirms that it was because of the ungodly practices of Sodom that God turned it into a smoldering heap of ash (2 Peter 2:6). Jude 1:7, 1 Corinthians 10:8, and 1 Thessalonians 4:3-6 also speak clearly against sexual immorality. Finally, Isaiah 3:8-9 says that Jerusalem and Judah were ruined because their sin was like that of Sodom. The people "rewarded evil unto themselves," and God carried them into captivity and allowed the Babylonians to scrape the city clean like scraps off a plate, (For yet another testimony about the perversion of Sodom, read Ezekiel 16:48.)

The perversion of God's good gift of sexuality is the first stage in incurring the wrath of God.

Stage Two: Social Perversion

When standards are perverted at the personal level, as in sexual perversion, it is only a matter of time before the whole society is perverted, according to Romans 1:28-31:

> And even as they did not like to retain God in their knowledge, God gave them over to a reprobate mind, to do those things which are not convenient; being filled with all unrighteousness, fornication, wickedness, covetousness, maliciousness; full of envy, murder, debate, deceit, malignity: whisperers, backbiters, haters of God, despiteful, proud, boasters, inventors of evil things, disobedient to parents, without understanding, covenantbreakers, without natural affection, implacable, unmerciful.

The world becomes a madhouse when we turn our backs on God, much as we are presently experiencing in every society on earth. We live in self-made cells and lock ourselves in at night while hoodlums roam up and down the streets. Our wives and daughters are afraid to go out at night and we have every imaginable form of violence and mayhem. It should be evident to all that God is allowing the human race to reap the results of turning our backs on Him.

Stage Three: Spiritual Perversion

Verse 32 reveals the final stage, spiritual perversion: "Who, knowing the judgment of God, that they which commit such things are worthy of death, not only do the same, but have pleasure in them that do them." We have begun to entertain ourselves with perversion. Television sitcoms and movies depict drunkenness and perversion, immorality and adultery, and every conceivable form of violence. Psychic networks lead people to fulfill any and all desires. And we give awards to the actors who emulate these perversions the most effectively!

Three times in this chapter Paul records God's response to those who turn away from Him: He gave them up (verse 24), He gave them up (verse 26), and He gave them over (verse 28). Do you know the very worst thing that God could do to America? Leave us alone. just give us over to our sins. We must pray that God will not turn His back on us, for the day He does our destruction will closely follow.

Will you examine your own heart for signs of willful self-determination, wicked self-deception, or woeful self-destruction? If you find even the slightest evidence, repent of it by turning and worshiping the true Creator God and receive His cleansing.

Application

1. Read John 8:9. What is one of the purposes of your conscience? *To keep you from sinning*

Read Acts 23:1. What role did Paul's conscience play in his life? *He lived with a good conscience toward God*

What was Paul's goal regarding his conscience (Acts 24:16)? *To avoid offence toward men and God.*

In Romans 2:15 and 9:1, Paul says the conscience "bears witness." Comparing this to a witness in a courtroom, what role does the conscience play? *There is a God,*

What can cause one's conscience to become pure over time (Hebrews 9:14)? *The blood of Jesus Christ through the Holy Spirit, cleanses our conscience*

2. Read Psalm 19:1-6. List the ways that creation manifests the Creator. What aspect of God's creation speaks most plainly to you of God's existence? *The heavens declare the glory of God and the firmament shows his creation. The way everything has order. The way man is made and animals + the cosmos,*

3. Cite a time when you suppressed, or held down, the truth of God in order to follow your own desires. *Getting angry, losing my temper, gossiping about others. fight with Roseann.*

What was the result of your actions? How did the Lord bring you to a place of yielding to His truth? *Getting into fights and causing others to be hurt. Broken relationship*

Read Acts 26:24-32. After hearing Paul's testimony, King Agrippa's answer to Paul indicates an avoidance of the issue of truth. What pressures could have caused Agrippa to suppress the truth? *afraid he would lose his position as king*

Read John 3:1-2. What did Nicodemus do to discover the truth from Jesus? *he came to Jesus at night and questioned wanted to know who he was*

What evidence was there that Nicodemus continued to allow the truth to flourish in his fife (John 7:50; 19:39)?

He helped in the burial and continued to believe in Jesus

4. Read 1 Corinthians 1:18-29. Why is it not always the smartest person who has the most truth? *God has chosen the foolish things of the world to confound the wise. Truth is not revealed through a high intelligence but by th Holy Spirit within a person.*

Read Luke 10:21. What does God do at times with His truth?

he hides things from the wise and reveals it to babes

Who are the "babes" or "little children" in this verse?

children of God who have faith as a child.

Could one be highly educated, but still be a "babe" or "little child" in God's sight? Why or why not?

only if they are born again and humble as a little child

5. What do you think are the most prevalent idols in American culture?

Hollywood, celebrities political figures. Wealthy people

What do you think are the idols in your life (that which tugs at your affections and is contrary to God's will)?

Vanity, Judgeing & critiqueing others, money

If you have not forsaken the idols that you identified, what could happen in your life in the long run?

my faith will be shipwreeked

Digging Deeper

Take a piece of paper and list the 23 characteristics of people who have been "given over" by God to the results of their sin (see Romans 1:29-31). Cite one or two specific examples from our culture. Then, on a scale of 1-10 (1 = mild, 10 = severe), assign a score for where you feel this practice is in our culture. [Note: this is not a scientific score, but rather your personal, subjective feeling about sin in our culture.] Finally, based on signs of a declining culture in Romans 1, what would you predict America's future to be over the next 10 years?

THE LAST STEP ON THE WAY DOWN

Overview

*God's laws without consequence are mere advice. Paul warns
the church in Romans 1 that ignoring God's principles of sexual
morality is a sure step toward serious consequences.*

Introduction: Romans 1:24

In our last lesson we saw how Paul illustrates a principle: it's
the bad news that makes the good news good. The bad news
Paul presents in Romans chapter 1 is how man suppresses
the truth about God, and how man's denial leads him deeper
into sin. So deep, in fact, that God finally releases mankind to
experience the results of his own sin. We're going to continue
that theme in this lesson but with a very specific application
tied to a fundamental institution in society: marriage.

The unbelievable assault on sexual purity in our country—even around the world—is the final step on the ladder that descends into the judgment of God. And this is the primary focus of Paul's "bad news" in Romans 1. Three times he says that God gives man over to the results of sexual impurity (Romans 1:24, 26, 28). So many of the things Paul mentions are the practices that are becoming more and more condoned in our society: homosexuality, fornication, vile affections, lust, and sexual uncleanness. When a nation loses the ability to govern itself in the realm of sexual morality, this leads to losses of control in every area of life.

Remarkably, Edward Gibbon wrote a huge set of books on *The Decline and Fall of the Roman Empire*, in which he cites the leading causes of the decline of the (then) world empire. Sexual immorality was at the top of his list, along with the mad craze for more brutal forms of entertainment, public spending, and the decline of religion. Sound familiar? It should, because those could be characteristics of our own culture. Will someone write *The Decline and Fall of the American Empire* someday, citing those same cracks in the mortar of our morality?

In an age where virtues are vanishing like the mist, a new virtue has taken center stage: the "virtue" of tolerance. And the only sin is to call sin a sin. Calling right "right" and wrong "wrong" is now considered narrow-minded, bigoted, and judgmental. To agree with what the Bible calls sin can land you in court on a charge of intolerance. So we are instituting morality by the majority and using public opinion as our guiding light.

Fortunately, we still have our Bibles. God's Word on sexual purity is still plain: "Neither shalt thou commit adultery" (Deuteronomy 5:18). After giving this and the other nine commandments, God says, "O that there were such an heart in them, that they would fear me, and keep all my commandments always, that it might be well with them, and with their children for ever!" (Deuteronomy 5:29). I can do what I can to protect my children and grandchildren from the deteriorating standards of our world, but it is getting harder and harder. And how hard will it be when the vestiges of prior generations are totally gone? It will be like it was in Israel when there were no longer any generations alive who knew the Lord or talked about His mighty works. And everyone began doing what was right in their own eyes.

The sexual revolution that began in the 1960s has borne its fruit. And unless the people of God take a stand against it they will be swept away in its results. The first line of cultural defense against sexual immorality is a strong marriage that is built on sexual purity. This is the only way children will have to measure what they see and hear in society. If they don't see God's ideal in the Christian family, where will they learn it?

Discussion

The Lord Jesus Christ put this matter of marriage fidelity right up front. He said in Matthew 19:5, "For this cause shall a man leave father and mother, and shall cleave to his wife: and they twain shall be one flesh?" Our Lord is saying that the underlying basis of all society is the home and the underlying basis of that is sexual fidelity in marriage.

Each partner in a marriage is to make their spouse their primary responsibility. If a wife makes the children her primary focus, and a husband makes his work or career his primary focus, then the marriage will suffer. And when the marriage suffers, sexual temptation becomes all-too-attractive. This is where so much immorality begins.

Dealing with sexual immorality in marriage—specifically, adultery—is of utmost importance in the Body of Christ. Otherwise, we will be hearing God say one day, "I give you over." No more frightful words could ever be spoken to an individual, culture, nation, or world. Let's look at the reasons why adultery is such a hellish sin in its action and its impact.

Adultery: A Sin Against One's Self

First, adultery is a sin against one's self First Corinthians 6:18 says, "Flee fornication." That is, get out of there! "Every sin that a man doeth is without the body; but he that commiteth fornication sinneth against his own body." Technically, fornication is sexual sin before marriage. But the remedy (flee!) and the results (sinning against one's self) are the same for adultery as for fornication.

How does one sin against his own body when he commits fornication or adultery? In every way. Psychologically, spiritually, and physically, one hurts himself. In the last ten years, nine times more people have died from sexually transmitted diseases than died in the worst ten years of the Vietnam War. While we hear a lot today about safe sex, it is not God's version of safe sex. The sex that God instituted is always safe because it is reserved for a life partner and that person exclusively.

Adultery: A Sin Against the Home

Second, adultery is a sin against the home. The most devastating thing that can happen to a child's future concept of sex is to learn that his/her parents had sex with other partners. The next most devastating thing that can influence a child's concept of sexual morality is for a person who is committing adultery to advocate sexual fidelity. This is a double bind message that confuses young people who are trying to sort out roles and responsibilities in life.

When a man commits adultery, he conveys a message to his children that their mother is not worth much and that he is not an honest man. The message says that pleasure is more important than principle. What a devastating message! Today's 40- and 50-year-old parents, who learned about sexual freedom in the '60s, have sent damaging messages to today's older teens and college students. It will take a miracle to get sexual morality back on track after the damage that has been done.

Adultery: A Sin Against the Church

Third, adultery is a sin against the church. Any believer who lives an impure life sins against the rest of the Body of Christ and specifically those in his local church fellowship. Paul says in 1 Corinthians 12:12 that "the body is one, and hath many members, and all the members of that one body, being many, are one body."

Therefore, if one member of the body sins, the whole body is hurt. What you do affects me, and what I do affects you.

Adultery is like an infection in the body, and the Body of Christ will never be healthy if there is hidden immorality in it.

I beg you, please, if there is immorality in your heart and in your life, get right or get out. Don't hurt the Body of Christ. Don't sing in the choir, play in the orchestra, sit on the platform, or preach from the pulpit, if this is your lifestyle. If you come to church, come to receive help, not to make a mockery of the holiness that we are to pursue. The ultimate problem is not that any of us have committed any sin—even the terrible sin of sexual immorality. The problem is that we continue in it and don't get help to put it away.

Adultery: A Sin Against the Nation

Fourth, adultery is a sin against the nation. It is not an overstatement to say that adultery is an act of treason. In the Old Testament, adultery was a crime punishable by death: "If a man be found lying with a woman married to an husband, then they shall both of them die, both the man that lay with the woman, and the woman" (Deuteronomy 22:22). Now listen to the rest of the verse: "So shalt thou put away evil from Israel." Put this sin not only away from the people of God, but from the nation itself.

It is foolish to say that character and leadership are not synonymous. No man is morally fit for leadership—at any level, but especially at the national level—who is sexually impure. Proverbs 14:34 says "Righteousness exalteth a nation: but sin is a reproach to any people." Character counts!

We're being told that the only thing that counts is the leader's skill. And that is true if you don't want God's blessing and help to fall upon that leader like a mantle. But what nation—especially one that has "In God We Trust" on its coinage—would want to live without the guidance and help of God? To have a morally impure leader is like having a surgeon who operates without scrubbing. Germs and bacteria touch everything that he touches.

We need leaders who are clean, so that all that they put their hands to can be blessed by God. Proverbs 16:12 says: "It is an abomination to kings to commit wickedness: for the throne is established by righteousness." Romans 13:4 says that public leaders are ministers of God. They are stewards, acting for God. Proverbs 20:28 says, "Mercy and truth preserve the king." Proverbs 31:3 is the advice that the mother of a king named Lemuel gave him. She said, "Give not thy strength unto women, nor thy ways to that which destroyeth kings."

Adultery at any level of a nation's life will infect the soul of the nation—even adultery by one person. But adultery or immorality at the top of a nation's leadership structure will flow downhill like molten lava, destroying everything in its path.

Adultery: A Sin Against God

Finally, adultery is a sin against Almighty God. To ask what difference sin makes is the same as asking what difference God makes. To break His statutes is to break His heart. Let's look at some Scriptures which make clear that immorality is a sin against God.

- Exodus 20:14 says, "Thou shalt not commit adultery." This sin is against God because God says it is wrong. It breaks one of His ten commandments.

- Praying to God, David said in Psalm 51:4, "Against thee, thee only, have I sinned, and done this evil in thy sight." David realized that when he committed adultery he broke both God's law, and God's heart, for his sin was against Almighty God.

- Hebrews 13:4: "Marriage is honourable in all, and the bed undefiled: but whoremongers and adulterers God will judge." I didn't say that—God said it.

- Proverbs 6:27-29: "Can a man take a fire in his bosom, and his clothes not be burned? Can one go upon hot coals, and his feet not be burned? So he that goeth in to his neighbour's wife; whosoever toucheth her shall not be innocent." Anyone thinking he or she can commit adultery and not be damaged is in a state of serious self-deception. God says they are guilty.

- Proverbs 6:32: "But whoso committeth adultery with a woman lacketh understanding: he that doeth it destroyeth his own soul." God warns us that adultery destroys the soul.

- Proverbs 7:27: "Her house is the way to hell, going down to the chambers of death." The adulteress' house is the doorway to hell. Walk through it and don't be surprised at what you find. You have been warned by God.

- 1 Corinthians 6:9: "Know ye not that the unrighteous shall not inherit the kingdom of God? Be not deceived: neither fornicators, nor idolaters, nor adulterers, nor effeminate, nor abusers of themselves with rnankind." God says don't be deceived; they're not going to heaven unless they change. Thank God Paul goes on to say, "And such were some of you" (1 Corinthians 6:11). Some of the Corinthians had changed, as anyone can who takes God's view of sin, repents, and receives His power to change.

- Ephesians 5:5: "For this ye know, that no whoremonger, nor unclean person, nor covetous man, who is an idolater, hath any inheritance in the kingdom of Christ and of God."

- Revelation 21:8: "But the fearful, and unbelieving, and the abominable, and murderers, and whoremongers, and sorcerers, and idolaters, and all liars, shall have their part in the lake which burneth with fire and brimstone: which is the second death." Whoremongers—the sexually immoral—find themselves among undesirable company in the lake of fire.

Does God take the sin of adultery seriously? Yes! We must take it as seriously as He does or suffer His response. God is a holy

God and has given us His commandments and laws. Law without penalty is only advice. God is not giving advice in His Word.

No matter how immorality is laughed at, glamorized, rationalized, or legitimized by the social engineers and the pundits, adultery is a sin that God will judge. Those who think they are getting away with it need only read Romans 2:5: "But after thy hardness and impenitent heart treasurest up unto thyself wrath against the day of wrath." If they don't experience wrath today, it is only because it is being stored up for the day of God's wrath. But wrath will come against sexual immorality, both corporately and individually.

What must the people of God do? "The time is come that judgment must begin at the house of God" (1 Peter 4:17). All Christians, but especially young people, need to take the following steps:

1. Make a decision. Give your heart to Almighty God, because He is the only one who is able to guide you.

2. Depend upon Him. He will deliver you from sexual immorality if you trust Him.

3. Be devoted. Love God with all of your heart and if you are married, love your spouse with a supernatural love. When the Bible says that husbands are to love their wives (Ephesians 5:25) and wives are to love their husbands (Titus 2:4), these are not suggestions. These are principles that represent the heart of God and they are to be obeyed.

4. Develop your relationship. Love is not like a diamond, something that you find. Love is like a flower, to be cultivated and nurtured. If you don't love your spouse more today than you did when you married him or her, you probably love your spouse less. Feed that love from day to day.

5. Be a disciple of marriage. Guard your company. Watch what you read and see. You wouldn't put garbage in your mouth, so don't put garbage in your mind.

6. Be determined. Joshua said, "but as for me and my house, we will serve the Lord" (Joshua 24:15). If you make up your mind about one big decision, you won't have to keep making up your mind about a lot of little decisions.

This has been a hard lesson, but one that is true and salted with God's love, grace, and forgiveness. The Gospel is the power of God unto salvation (Romans 1:16). No sin is too big for God to forgive; no hurt is too deep for God to heal. His power looks for a place to be applied today. If your heart and life are that place, receive His grace and His power today.

Application

1. Read Genesis 39:6-12. Describe how Joseph fulfilled the admonition of 1 Corinthians 6:18. *He fled from the temptation to fornicate, he fled youthful lust.*

   What do you learn about Joseph's thinking and priorities from Genesis 39:9? *He put God first and thought also how it would affect Potipher.*

What evidence is there in verse 10 that Joseph's resolve was strong? *He resisted the temptation*

State in your own words what you believe the standard was that Joseph had established for himself regarding sexual purity.

He would reserve sex for marriage only.

What evidence do you see that Joseph had established personal standards before the incident with Potiphar's wife arose? *He said he wouldn't sin against God*

Write out your own personal standards for sexual purity.

No sex before marriage

What are the advantages to establishing personal standards for purity before temptation arises?

When temptation arises you can resist the devil and sin

2. Read Genesis 2:24 and Matthew 19:5. What does it mean to become "one flesh"?

You become one in body and spirit.

Read Matthew 19:6. When Jesus says "let not man put asunder," what does He mean?

Nothing or no person should come between the relationship to destroy or separate the couple.

Why did Jesus instruct men not to undo something God has done? What harm could result?

Man messes up God's plans by trusting his way of doing things. If could destroy your life.

3. Read 1 Corinthians 12:26. How does the Body of Christ experience the truth of this verse, in both positive and negative ways? *We are all connected and when one believer sins it affects everyone*

What are some of the most obvious sexual sins that are committed by members of the Body of Christ in our society?
fornication, adultery, homosexuality,

What impact are these sins having on the church as a whole?
It is weakening it's witness and effectiveness

What do we do to save a human body from a cancerous growth that is attacking and weakening it? How would you apply that metaphor to the Body of Christ? (Read (Read 1 Corinthians 5:1-11.) *Don't associate with them pray for them*

Have you seen the church take action against sexual sin? If so, how do you feel it was handled? *Could have been handled better*

What impact do you think stronger action by church leaders might have on purity in the Body of Christ? Read Matthew 18:15-17. How should church leadership handle occasions of sexual sin? *tell it to the person who sinned then bring it to church leaders 2 or 3 if he doesn't listen, If he doesn't listen then he should not be allowed in church*

4. Read Ecclesiastes 5:4-5. How does this apply to keeping the bonds of marriage? *Don't get married if you can't keep your vows to spouse*

What is the "payment" that is required of couples who agree to be married? What is the "cost" in the realm of sexual activity? *be committed for life, Don't commit adultery stay faithful to each other.*

If the "cost" of marriage is giving up illicit sexual activity, what is the "gain" that is received by couples who remain faithful to one another? *They have a marriage that stays together.*

Digging Deeper

Do your own personal study on the pervasiveness of sexual themes in our culture. With your spouse or a mature friend, watch a half-dozen of the most popular weeknight television sitcoms or relationship-oriented dramas. Catalog the number of sexual innuendoes and references made in each show, including the use of sexually explicit slang and terms. For the second part of your research, watch via cable TV channels, video compilations (for rent in video stores), or other sources several TV shows from the 1950s and 1960s, looking for the same statistics. Compare your findings, and draw your own conclusions about the trends of our culture's morality. How can you personally, and for your family, take a stand against this cultural shift in mores?

HOW GOD HANDLES HYPOCRITES

Overview

How much truth is there in the lives of most people? Are we seeing a mask, or the real person? Often, we don't know. But one Person does. Paul warns hypocrites that their double life will one day be revealed and judged.

Introduction: Romans 2:1-8, 16

An archaeologist named Howard Carter discovered the tomb of the Egyptian King Tut back in the early 1920s. When he finally broke into the tomb, he went in and found the casket, the sarcophagus. I have seen this huge casket in the Egyptian museum, and it is as beautiful as it is large.

When he opened the outer casket, he discovered another casket inside, and then a third casket inside the second. Each of these was covered with gold leaf, as ornate as could be imagined.

When the fourth casket was opened, Carter discovered the mummy of King Tut, buried with the beautiful solid gold mask which has been seen in so many pictures over the years. But, despite all of this outward beauty, when Carter removed the solid gold death mask from the head of King Tut, inside was nothing but a dry, dusty, lifeless corpse. What is true for all humanity was also true for the great Egyptian king—outer beauty can conceal, but cannot change, inner death.

In this lesson, we look at Paul's words in Romans about hypocrites, those who go through life with a mask, concealing their true selves underneath. Unfortunately, hypocrites think they are also hiding their true selves from God, but they are not. God will one day reveal the truth about every sinner, especially those who think they have been fooling God all of their life. And that is Paul's message.

In Romans 2, Paul addresses a group of religious people who supported his strong message of God's judgment to the heathen. These Zealots were indignant at the sins of others but indulgent about their own. Paul's theme in Romans 2 is judgment, as he expresses in verse 1: "Therefore thou art inexcusable, 0 man, whosoever thou art that judgest: for wherein thou judgest another, thou condemnest thyself; for thou that judgest doest the same things." The religious, self-righteous person who believes that God's judgment is going to fall only on the heathen has a surprise coming. Paul makes it clear that the surprise is their own judgment:

- Verse 2: "the judgment of God."
- Verse 3: "the judgment of God."
- Verse 5: "the righteous judgment of God."
- Verse 16: "God shall judge."

Paul has a message for those who think God's judgment is only for others. Let's look closely at what the message is.

Discussion

What is the judgment of the hypocrite going to be like? God's judgment on the self-righteous sinner will be "according to" three things: truth (verse 2), deeds (verse 6), and the Gospel (verse 16), which form the basis of God's judgment.

God's Judgment Is According to Truth

First of all, the judgment is going to be according to truth, and therefore there will be no disguise. In the Greek language, the word hypocrite means actor, or to play a part. And in the days of Greek theater, the actors would wear masks to convey the feeling of their character. A smiling mask would convey happiness, a frowning mask would convey sadness, and a fierce mask would convey anger.

Paul's message here is that there will be a day when the masks are taken off and the truth is revealed. It will not be the pretense that is judged, but the reality.

In our day we have begun to value knowledge over truth. We can have intellectuals who are not honest. It has been said that, for comparative purposes, all the knowledge gained in the world from creation through 1845 would measure one inch if stacked on a table. The next century's increase, to 1945, would have grown to three inches high. In thirty years, by 1975, the stack of knowledge would be as high as the Washington Monument. But the knowledge gained since 1975 would be represented by a stack reaching out of sight into the sky. That's how much knowledge has increased. (See Daniel 12:4 for an insight on the increase of knowledge!)

But does becoming smarter lead to becoming more truthful? Not according to 2 Timothy 3:5-7, where Paul describes those "having a form of godliness ... ever learning, and never able to come to the knowledge of the truth." Everything God does is based on truth: the Word (Ephesians 1:13), the Spirit (John 14:17), the church (1 Timothy 3:15), and His Son (John 14:6).

Though truth has fallen in the streets today, the hypocrite's judgment is going to stand firm. God knows the truth and He will judge every hypocrite by the truth, no matter what office he holds, fame he enjoys, or prestige he has achieved. Truth is to your spirit what food is to your body, what light is to your eyes, what melody is to your ears. It is essential and liberating to make life worth living!

Now, because the hypocrite doesn't understand that God is going to judge according to truth, he makes three fatal mistakes in his thinking:

Mistake #1: Appearance Is All that Matters

The hypocrite believes that somehow what he presents on the outside is all that matters. Jesus' words to the Pharisees in Matthew 23:25-28 address this point specifically. I want you to see how pointedly Jesus speaks to this issue of appearance:

> Woe unto you, scribes and Pharisees, hypocrites! for ye make clean the outside of the cup and of the platter, but within they are full of extortion and excess. Thou blind Pharisee, cleanse first that which is within the cup and platter, that the outside of them may be clean also. Woe unto you, scribes and Pharisees, hypocrites! for ye are like unto whited sepulchers, which indeed appear beautiful outward, but are within full of dead men's bones, and of all uncleanness. Even so ye also outwardly appear righteous unto men, but within ye are full of hypocrisy and iniquity.

This sounds like the burial of King Tut. Gold on the outside, dead bones and dust on the inside. Isn't this what Paul is addressing in Romans 2: 21-23?

> Thou therefore which teachest another, teachest thou not thyself? thou that preachest a man should not steal, dost thou steal? Thou that sayest a man should not commit adultery, dost thou commit adultery? thou that abhorrest idols, dost thou commit sacrilege? Thou that makest thy boast of the law, through breaking the law dishonourest thou God?

In the Beatitudes, Jesus settled the question of whether outward obedience is the same as inward obedience. Hate and lust in the heart are the same as murder and adultery by the hand (Matthew 5:21-28). The hypocrite makes a tragic mistake when he believes that the dead spiritual bones inside of him will never be seen. Someday God will expose them all on the basis of truth.

Mistake #2: Lack of Trouble Means I'm Right With God

There's a second mistake that the hypocrite makes. He thinks that if he is not being chastised, if he's not having trouble, he's right with God. Look in Romans 2:3-4:

> *And thinkest thou this, O man, that judgest them which do such things, and doest the same, that thou shalt escape the judgment of God? Or despisest thou the riches of his goodness and forbearance and long-suffering; not knowing that the goodness of God leadeth thee to repentance?*

Some people have the idea that if they're not having any problems, they're right with God. If they're healthy and have money in the bank, evidently God loves them and they are living a clean life before God. Friend, the blessings of God don't mean that you're right with God. God gives you blessings to bring you to Him. It doesn't mean you are walking without sin and don't need daily repentance. Romans 2:4 says that the goodness of God leads to repentance.

I want to remind you that Sodom and Gomorrah, which we discussed in our last lesson, were in an economic all-time high when the fire and brimstone fell. There was so much prosperity that the people were full of bread and idleness. But the fire fell because they did not respond to the goodness of God. On two occasions in Jesus' day, terrible tragedies took place where people were killed (Luke 13:1-5). When questioned about the sinfulness of those killed, Jesus said that wasn't the issue. The issue is you need to repent and be right with God while you're alive!

Mistake #3: Delayed Judgment Means No Judgment

Romans 2:5 says that wrath is being treasured up by the hypocrite against the day of God's judgment. Delayed judgment means nothing except that the eventual judgment is going to be worse! When God blesses a nation or an individual and that country or person hardens its heart against God, they are just putting wrath in the bank.

Why doesn't God judge right away? Because God waits for all of that sin to ripen. You put it in the bank and at the judgment you collect it with compound interest. When you sin against God, your sin does not just end here, it goes on and on and on and the ripples touch the shores of eternity. The hypocrite does not escape his sins. Paul says in verse 3: "thinkest thou shalt escape?" The word *think* is a technical word; the phrase means, "Have you figured out a way to escape? Do you think that somehow you're going to escape the judgment of God?" You can't do it!

Outward appearance, a peaceful life, and no judgment does not mean that the truth will not ultimately be revealed. God will one day judge according to truth. But He also judges according to deeds.

God's Judgment Is According to Deeds

Romans 2:6 says, "Who will render to every man according to his deeds." You see, you're not saved by works but you will be judged by works. And God is no respecter of persons (verse 11). Paul will show in Romans 3 that the whole world is guilty before God, and every person will be judged ultimately according to his/her deeds.

Sometimes when I am interviewed I will be asked, "Do you think a Jew without Jesus is lost?" The interviewer tries to put me in a hot box. If you say "No," you defame the Gospel. If you say "Yes," you're a racist and a bigot. I always answer this way: "One of my own children without Jesus is lost. It's not a matter of face, race, or place, it's a matter of grace. If you have received the grace of God in Christ, you are saved regardless of who you are. If you haven't received the grace of God in Christ, you aren't saved regardless of who you are."

God's standard is perfection. If we haven't kept the whole law, but have sinned in just one part, we are lost (see James 2:10). It's as if we're hanging over a fire by a chain with ten links. Nine of the links are made of steel and one of crepe paper. Just one link—that's all it takes for us to perish. The breaking of even one of God's ten commandments will be the deed upon which we are judged.

Our deeds are viewed by God in three different ways:

God Judges By Actions

The deeds mentioned in Romans 2:6 are just that—actions, works, what we do and don't do. Sins of commission, sins of omission, sins of the flesh, and sins of the spirit. All of us have committed sinful actions which will be judged by God.

God Judges By Attitudes

Romans 2:7-8 deals with several attitudes: contentious, not obeying the truth, and unrighteous. The hypocrite who has an attitude that is against God will find those attitudes judged by Him. Some people just look for things to criticize in life. They are contentious, have a mean streak, and always seem to be against God and everybody else. And because they are looking for those things in life, they find them wherever they go—especially in church. Some blame their lack of faith or obedience on God, saying if He were different they would believe in Him. God will judge that attitude.

God Judges By Advantages

It is true that some people in life have more advantages than others, and God is going to take that into account when He judges. Romans 2:9-10 points out that judgment and blessing come first to the Jew and then to the Gentile. Why is that? Because the Jew has had the advantage. Romans 3:1 says that because the truth of God was first delivered to the Jew, they have had the advantage.

Jesus said it another way, "But he that knew not, and did commit things worthy of stripes shall be beaten with few stripes. For unto whomsoever much is given, of him shall be much required: and to whom men have committed much, of him they will ask the more" (Luke 12:48).

God holds you responsible for what you read in your Bible, for what you hear in your church service or Bible study meeting, and even for the truth you are reading in this study guide. There are millions of people on earth who sit in darkness because they have never heard the name of Jesus. It would be sad to go to hell from the jungle, but how much sadder it would be to go to hell from an air conditioned, upholstered church pew. How sad it would be to sing in the choir and go to hell. How sad it would be to be an usher and go to hell. How sad it would be to sit on the platform and go to hell. Jesus said, "Many will say to me in that day, Lord, have we not prophesied in thy name? and in thy name have cast out devils? and in thy name done many wonderful works? And then will I profess unto them, I never knew you: depart from me, ye that work iniquity" (Matthew 7:22-23).

God's Judgment Is According to the Gospel

Finally, God will judge according to the Gospel: "In the day when God shall judge the secrets of men by Jesus Christ, according to my gospel" (Romans 2:16). First Corinthians 15:1-4 tells us what the Gospel is: "Christ died for our sins, . . . that he was buried, and that he rose again the third day according to the Scriptures." That, friend, is Gospel truth. And if that Gospel does not save you, that Gospel will judge you because that is the Gospel of the resurrection of Jesus Christ. It is the resurrected Christ who will one day be our judge (John 5:22).

Friend, what you are about to read is the most important truth you will learn in this lesson. You're going to meet Jesus Christ. If you do not meet Jesus Christ in salvation, you'll meet Him in judgment. If the Gospel does not save you, the Gospel will condemn you. In Acts 17:31: "he hath appointed a day, in which he will judge the world in righteousness by that man whom he hath ordained; whereof he hath given assurance unto all men, in that he hath raised him from the dead." What does that mean? That means that the resurrection of Jesus Christ which is meant to save you is the very resurrection that will condemn you.

Make sure today that the resurrection of Jesus Christ, and the judgment which God has put on His shoulders, are truths that bring life, not death, to you!

Application

1. Read Luke 6:42 and Matthew 7:4-5. What is the "hypocrite" in these verses doing? *looking out the sins weaknesses in a person and judging*

    What is the "beam"? *the sin in our own life.*

What is Jesus communicating by comparing a "speck" or "mote" in one person's eye to the "beam" or "log" in the hypocrite's eye? Who really has the larger problem?

take care of your own sin before you judge some one else the person who is judging another

And what is the hypocrite's problem? *they do the same and have same sin as the one they are judging*

What might be a practical truth for you to remember whenever you feel like trying to "fix" something in someone else's life? *Work on your self first.*

2. Read Luke 13:11-17. Why were the Jewish leaders critical of Jesus? *Because he healed a woman on the Sabbath.*

What was the reaction of the hypocrites (verse 17)?

they were ashamed,

What was the reaction of the observers (verse 17)?

they rejoiced at what Jesus did,

How obvious is it to others when hypocrisy is present?

Very obvious

3. Describe a time when you acted hypocritically. That is, you criticized someone for doing something that you yourself have done. *not being kind and being enuious*

How did you feel when you realized your hypocrisy?

guilty and convicted

4. Under the three bases for judgment mentioned in the lesson (actions, attitudes, advantages), evaluate your own life. If the judgment of God were to fall today, how would you be judged?

    • Actions for which I believe I would be judged:

    vanity judging and critiqueing others

    • Attitudes for which I believe I would be judged:

    Pride, thinking more highly of myself than I ought, unbelief, resentment

    • Spiritual advantages for which I believe I would be held accountable:

    having spiritual gift of tongues

If by the end of today the judgment of God has not come, what do you think you should do about those items you've listed above? *Repent*

Having identified the areas of life which need correcting, how will the eventual judgment of God be different if you continue in them and don't deal with them today?

Things will get worse

Digging Deeper

There is irony in the judgment of hypocrisy. For an excercise in etymology (the origin of words), look up "hypocrisy" in a large dictionary. You'll discover that it comes from a compound Greek word, *hypo* + *krisis*, which originated from a word meaning to explain, or ... to judge! You see, when we act hypocritically, we choose to judge a situation and explain it to our advantage. We decide how we want it to appear and put on the appropriate mask. My friend, there is a greater Judge waiting in the wings who will one day rip off all the masks. How much wiser for us to judge ourselves now in the way He will judge!

GOD VS. HUMANITY

Overview

*For those who think God isn't fair, Paul the apostle becomes
prosecuting attorney and reveals the truth. God isn't fair. But
He is just. And it is justice, and His offer of mercy, that can save
every guilty sinner.*

Introduction: Romans 3:9-10

W e're studying together the Constitution of Christianity,
the book of Romans, the greatest piece of literature
ever written. Romans tells us about the solution to the greatest
problem in the world—sin. We are into the third chapter of
Romans in this lesson, but still have not begun to look in detail
at the cure, because Paul is still explaining the sickness. As
we've said before, bad news is what makes good news good,
and Paul is making sure that we understand the gravity of sin.

You may think that Paul is morose, cruel, or vindictive
when he writes on and on about sin. We have a generation today

that doesn't want to hear much about this topic, but if you study Romans you're going to hear it.

First of all, Paul talked in chapter one about the sin of the heathen—those who've never heard. Then in chapter two he talked about the sin of the hypocrites—those who have heard but whose lives are full of duplicity. And then in the last part of chapter two he talks about the sin of the Hebrews—those who thought that because they were God's chosen people that somehow sin did not affect them. So after he deals with the sin of the heathen and the hypocrites and the Hebrews, he sums it up in chapter three with the sin of humanity. He says there's no difference between the Jew and the Greek, for all have sinned and come short of the glory of God.

As Paul begins Romans 3, you realize that what he is doing is setting up a courtroom scene. He positions himself as the prosecuting attorney who brings the human race up to the judgment bar of Almighty God. God vs. humanity. The evidence will be overwhelming. We will be found guilty. And judgment will be pronounced. But at the end of the trial, the Judge makes a surprise move that saves all who want to be saved.

Discussion

The Indictment

The indictment is found in Romans 3:9-10: "What then? are we better than they? [better than the heathen, better than the hypocrite, better than the Hebrew?] No, in no wise: for we have before proved both Jews and Gentiles, that they are all under sin; as it is written, There is none righteous, no, not one."

Now the words "under sin" literally mean dominated by sin, ruled by sin, and subjugated to sin. It is not only that we sin but we also serve sin—we become slaves of sin. We are free to do what we want but we're not free to do as we ought. This indictment extends to every class of person in the world. From the perspective of Judaism in Paul's day, there were two classes: Jews and everybody else (non-Jews, or Gentiles).

A comparison game is inevitable, but the standard is the glory of God. Paul says in verse 23 that "all have sinned, and come short of the glory of God." When non-Christians resist going to church by saying they are already as good as those Christians, they've got it all wrong. They're as bad as those Christians! All of us are totally depraved, totally infected by the disease of sin. And no amount of reformation or church attendance will cure it. Lay a twisted oak on a giant saw and cut off the twisted outer portions and you'll still see twisted heartwood running through the middle. Straightening up the outside doesn't straighten up the inside.

The Evidence

First, man is indicted: Guilty of total depravity. But what evidence does Paul, the prosecutor, bring to the courtroom to justify the indictment?

Man's Corrupted Wisdom

First of all, he talks about man's corrupted wisdom. Look in Romans 3:11: "There is none that understandeth." Man's mind has been warped by sin. Paul has also told us in 1 Corinthians 2:14 that, "the natural man receiveth not the things of the Spirit of God: for they are foolishness unto him: neither can he know them, because they are spiritually discerned." Even a man with a Ph.D. cannot understand God on his own.

The brilliance of mankind is everywhere around us. Computers, medicine, space travel—it's almost inconceivable. But when it comes to spiritual and eternal things, man is an ignoramus. The average man thinks he can go to heaven without being born again. He's absolutely ignorant of two things: he doesn't know how sinful he is and he doesn't know how holy God is. His wisdom is corrupt.

Man's Corrupted Will

But not only has his mind been corrupted by sin; his will has been corrupted as well. The second half of verse 11 says it best: "There is none that seeketh after God." You would think that men might seek God, but this verse says that they don't. Not the true God, anyway. Mankind all over the world seeks the gods of their own imaginations, the gods that cater to their own vices. But they do not seek the holy God of the Bible.

The only reason that anyone begins moving in God's direction is because God first seeks them out. Ever since the Garden of Eden, man has been running from God. Adam sinned and hid from God, and God sought him out. God has been seeking out sinners ever since. The Bible makes it clear that we love Him because He first loved us (1 John 4:19). Jesus said in John 6:44, "No man can come to me, except the Father which hath sent me draw him."

We hear a lot today about "seeker services" in churches as a means for reaching the lost. But the Bible tells us who the real Seeker is. His name is Jesus. Luke 19:10 says, "The Son of man is come to seek and to save that which was lost." Isn't that great? We need to be sensitive to those who are seeking to know more of Christ, at the same time recognizing that God is the true seeker of the lost. One thing about a sheep is, he never says, "Oh, I'm lost, I've got to go back to the shepherd." If the shepherd doesn't go and find him, he will never come home.

Finally, in Romans 3:12, Paul says that every person has "gone out of the way"—not doing any good at all. "Unprofitable" in the Greek referred to milk or meat that was spoiled. It is good for nothing except to be thrown out.

Man's Corrupted Words

What would you expect on the outside of someone who had corrupt wisdom and a corrupt will on the inside? Probably corrupt words, which is Paul's next piece of evidence that "all have sinned, and come short of the glory of God" (Romans 3:23). Romans 3:13-14 point out that man's throat is like a grave (meaning his words produce death), his words are deceitful, poisonous, and full of cursing and bitterness. Is that true? We know it is true of the rougher strata of life where language and words are used without restraint. But we discover by occasional disclosures that even those in the highest levels of government or industry use their speech to accomplish personal agendas. Tape recordings made of the conversations of a modern American president proved ultimately to turn public sentiment against him so that he had to leave office. The coarseness and evil intent of his words were more than the public could take (although his words are mild compared to what is heard today).

It goes beyond saying that evil speech is simply a barometer of the heart. Did not Jesus say that "those things which proceed out of the mouth come forth from the heart; and they defile the man" (Matthew 15:18)? Evil speech is everywhere now. There is no form of profanity that has not been heard on network television, not to mention in movies. The "bleeps" that are employed to keep us from hearing the words do little to protect us from the depraved mind of the speaker. We know what they say and what they mean.

Man's Corrupted Ways

Romans 3:15-17 moves ahead with further evidence of depravity, this time in describing man's corrupt ways: "Their feet are swift to shed blood: destruction and misery are in their ways: and the way of peace have they not known." Read any newspaper today, across the land or around the world. Violence, child abuse, abortion, war, and filth. Man's wicked ways have turned this world into a madhouse. This piece of evidence needs less explanation or illustration than any other. If we don't see it in the mirror we will see it on the evening news or the afternoon talk show.

Man's Corrupted Worship

The indictment continues, this time with a piece of evidence that may be the root of all the others. Man does not fear God (Romans 3:18). After being named guilty of all the other previously named sins, you would think that mankind would be prostrate on the ground, saying, "Oh, God, have mercy." Not Paul's generation and not ours! The world is littered with egomaniacs, strutting towards hell, laughing about God. The fear of God—a reverent, holy awe toward Almighty God— is the beginning of wisdom (Proverbs 1:7). Many have never discovered the fear of God.

In summary, Paul is saying that the worst form of badness is human goodness exercised apart from God. There really is nothing that man can do that is not tainted by sin. That is the meaning of total depravity. Not that we are as bad as we could be, but everything we do is tainted with badness. In the court of God, though man does some "good" things, they are still evidence of sin and depravity when they are not done with the ultimate goal of glorifying Him. Paul rests his case with this overwhelming evidence.

The Verdict

Mankind has been indicted by God, and His prosecuting attorney Paul has presented the evidence. What is the verdict? It is found in Romans 3:19-20:

> *Now we know that what things soever the law saith, it saith to them who are under the law: that every mouth may be stopped, and all the world may become guilty before God. Therefore by the deeds of the law there shall no flesh be justified in his sight: for by the law is the knowledge of sin.*

The verdict of the court is "guilty." We have been condemned by the Law of God that sets forth His perfect standards. The law was not given to save us; the law is given to condemn and convict us. God has given His holy laws but the law is given to show us that we're sinners, for sin is the transgression of the law. If we realize that God has given His holy law and that we have come short of His law, what is the wisest thing we could do? Close our mouths and plead guilty: "that every mouth may be stopped" (verse 19). We're never going to be saved until we stop our excuses and admit our guilt before Almighty God.

Remember the story in Luke 18:10-14 about the Pharisee and the publican, both of whom were praying before God? If Luke did not tell us which one was right before God, Romans 3 will. The Pharisee prayed about how good he was and how bad the publican was. The publican agreed with God that he was a sinner. It's people who agree with God that get saved. Paul says, "Shut your mouth, plead guilty." The verdict of the court is handed down.

The Mercy of God

I said at the beginning of this lesson that God, the Judge, makes a surprise move at the end toward those who want to be saved from their guilty verdict. His move is to extend mercy toward those who will receive it.

His mercy is not based on fairness, but on justice. The Judge knows that the penalty for the guilty must be paid, and He makes arrangements to do just that. If He were being fair, all would be condemned forever. So He is not being fair, He is being just. If you spend your time whining about God not being fair—about being mean and condemning you for your sins—you will never see His justice or receive His mercy. It is only when you agree with Him about your sins that you are able to receive His mercy.

Paul says later in Romans, "Whosoever shall call upon the name of the Lord shall be saved" (10:13). Have you seen your sin? Have you called out for His mercy? Have you received His mercy? If you can answer "Yes" to those questions, you are saved. If you answer "No," or don't know how to answer, you are not saved and I invite you now to plead for His mercy and ask forgiveness for your sins. "Yes" to the mercy of God is the only thing that saves a guilty sinner. The publican in Luke 18 set the standard: "God be merciful to me a sinner!" (verse 13).

Paul concludes his argument by summarizing the key elements of the righteousness and mercy of God that replaces the sinfulness of man. He does it with five prepositions found in Romans 3:22 and 24. God's justice is complete and sufficient because it fulfills the requirements of His own righteous law.

Righteousness of God

Only God can purify man's unclean soul. Righteousness is of God. Justification is the way that God declares us righteous in His sight. He puts the righteousness of Christ on our account and places our sin on Jesus' account. No one but God can do this. No one but Jesus can save us.

Righteousness By Faith

We exercise faith every day, but when things get tough we often become hesitant about placing our total faith in Christ. It is the only way to receive God's righteousness as a gift, by faith (see Ephesians 2:8-9). We must believe we have received His righteousness.

Righteousness Unto All

Jew or Gentile, it doesn't matter. Since all have sinned, righteousness is needed by, and available to, all. There is nobody so good that he doesn't need to be saved, and nobody so bad that he can't be saved. It is for all (see 2 Peter 3:9).

Righteousness By Grace

Grace is the most beautiful word in the Bible other than Jesus. It is grace that makes God love the unlovely. We are not loved because we're valuable, we're valuable because we're loved. We are saved, not by our works, but by His grace (2 Timothy 1:9). And we're loved by grace.

Righteousness In Christ

"Being justified freely by his grace through the redemption that is in Christ Jesus" (Romans 3:24). Jesus Christ is the key to our redemption, to God's justice, and to His offer of mercy. If Jesus had not fulfilled the righteous demands of the Law by dying for our sin, the Law would have sentenced us to hell. Jesus made it possible for God to be just instead of fair, and for us to be saved.

Paul concludes by showing us that God is both just and the justifier of everyone who believes in Jesus (Romans 3:26). The question now is, are you among the justified? Are you among those who have seen their sin, closed their mouths in their own defense, and asked for and received the mercy of God in Christ? I pray you will not read another word until you know that you are.

Application

1. Read Psalm 14:1-3 and 53:1-3, and compare them with Romans 3:10-12. What parallels do you find?

   They all say there is none righteous they don't seek God.

   Why do you think Paul went back to the Old Testament to find evidence of man's sinfulness?

   To show it was from the beginning of mankind.

   What does Psalm 53:1 call a person who says there is no God?

   A fool

Name an intellectual with whom you are impressed, but who also says "there is no God." What does Psalm 53:1 call this person?

he calls them a fool and corrupt.

How does this change your perception of that person?

They are spiritually dead.

Have you known someone you thought was not a Christian, but was a person who was exceptionally "good"? What do these verses say about that person's goodness?

If they are become filthy and corrupt and none is good

2. Read Proverbs 1:18. For whose lives do the wicked lie in wait and lay ambushes?

their own lives

Do the wicked often succeed in their plans? How is it, then, that they ultimately end up entrapping themselves?

They succeed but end up in destruction.

What role does depravity play in their spiritual blindness? Does a blind man know, on his own, that he is blind?

They can't see their sin and are blinded to the truth.

3. Read Acts 9:1-5. What was Paul's purpose for going to Damascus when Christ confronted him?

to kill any christian

Whose interests was Paul seeking to protect, God's or his Judaic reputation?

his Jewish reputation

Had Christ not intervened in Paul's life, what do you think would have happened to him? *He would have gone to Hell!*

How does Paul's story in Acts 9 illustrate the truth of John 15:16a? *God chose Paul that he would be a witness to the Gentiles to spread the gospel*

4. What do you learn about the mercy of God from 1 Timothy 1:13? *he is very merciful*

What do you learn from 1 Timothy 1:16? *God gives mercy to show his longsuffering as a witness to unbeliever's who will get saved.*

If God extended mercy to Paul in his pre-Christian days, will He extend mercy to you? *Yes, absolutely*

When and how did you first come to see your sin and call out for the mercy of God? *when I was 17 + 18yrs old*

What hope for yourself did you have outside of His mercy? *none*

What word does Titus 3:5 use to picture the effects of God's mercy in your life? *not by works but by God's mercy he saved me.*

Digging Deeper

With a little background help from the life of Zaccheus (Luke 19:2-8; evidence that tax collectors grew rich unscrupulously), examine the tax collector in Luke 18:9-14. Make two columns on a piece of paper. Label one "the Pharisee," the other "the tax collector." From Luke 18, write down all the descriptions offered in the passage, and your insights about the two men. Your primary focus is to compare their outer righteousness with their inner righteousness, and the place that mercy occupied in their thinking. What conclusions can you draw to apply to your own life?

IT'S TIME FOR SOME GOOD NEWS

Overview

Paul uses heroes of faith to show how God not only adds righteousness to the account of a sinful one, but adds sin to the account of the Righteous One. These transactions, while free for us, cost God the life of His Son.

Introduction: Romans 4:1

P reachers never get tired of telling the story of John Newton, the hymn writer who lived hundreds of years ago. Though he wrote many hymns, books, and sermons in his lifetime, we know him best as the author of the hymn "Amazing Grace." What most people don't know is the life John Newton lived before he wrote this timeless hymn, a life from which he was saved by God's amazing grace.

As a youngster, John Newton was rebellious and ungodly, and he left home at an early age to become a sailor like his father. Before too many years passed, Newton was involved in the African slave trade, and became a slave of slaves himself. He was kept chained to his mistress' table and given only scraps to eat. By God's providence, a copy of Thomas a Kempis' book *The Imitation of Christ* came into his hands—and he began to read it. One day during a ferocious storm at sea, a huge wave washed John Newton overboard, and he cried out to God for mercy. Miraculously, another huge wave came up and washed him back aboard the ship! That's all it took for John Newton to get right with God, and he served him as a preacher and writer in his native England for many years after that.

When John Newton wrote about amazing grace, he knew what he was talking about. That someone as evil and vile as Newton—a trafficker in human slave cargo—can be softened by the love of Christ is a miracle of grace if anything can be. John Newton is a perfect example of what we have been studying in Romans—that the bad news is what makes the good news good. Newton had heard plenty of bad news—he was bad news!—and so when he discovered the good news of the grace of God, he embraced it readily.

Now, we are going to study the good news of the grace of God in Romans. In chapters one through three, Paul has preached the bad news—that every person is under the condemnation of sin. Everyone! Hebrews, hypocrites, and all humanity. He summarized the bad news in Romans 3:23 by saying that "all have sinned, and come short of the glory of God." But in chapter four we are introduced to grace, the antidote to sin.

Before we begin this lesson, let me give you a definition of grace. It is the unmerited favor and kindness of God shown to one who does not deserve it and can never earn it. No one is saved apart from the grace of God. The only way to get it is to receive it by faith.

Discussion

In this lesson we are going to see the gospel according to three men: Abraham (the grace he discovered), David (the grace he described), and Paul (the grace he discloses).

The Grace Abraham Discovered

Paul begins his explanation of grace in Romans 4:1-3 by citing Abraham as an illustration:

> What shall we say then that Abraham our father, as pertaining to the flesh, hath found? For if Abraham were justified by works, he hath whereof to glory; but not before God. For what saith the scripture? Abraham believed God, and it was counted unto him for righteousness.

The words "hath found" come from the Greek word from which our word "eureka" comes: "I have found (it)!" It speaks of a discovery made by Abraham. And I note that Paul speaks of "Abraham our father." Abraham was the father of the Jewish nation, the first Hebrew, the founder of the Jewish faith, Abraham set the pattern and standard for a relationship with God, and if anyone could get to heaven on the basis of good works it would have been Abraham. And that is exactly the point Paul wants to make—he didn't get there by works, but by grace through faith.

Paul says, quoting Genesis 15:6, that Abraham believed God, and as a result of his faith, he was declared righteous by God. Abraham was called by God from a pagan background at an elderly age. He had no children, and he and his wife Sarah were beyond the childbearing age. Yet Cod came to Abraham and told him that he would become the father of millions of descendants! As many as the stars in the sky and the grains of sand on the seashore. For a couple who were too old to have even one child, this seemed preposterous on the surface. Yet Genesis records, and Paul reminds us, that Abraham believed God.

What did he believe God for? Well, he believed God for a miracle son. He believed that God would do what He said—somehow. And because Abraham put simple, childlike faith in the word of God, God counted it to him as righteousness (Genesis 15:6).

Why did God count it to Abraham as righteousness? I believe there were two reasons: because Abraham's faith gave honor and glory to God, and because Abraham received God's gift for what it was—the unmerited favor and kindness of God to one who didn't deserve it and could never earn it.

Salvation By Grace Respects God's Glory

In Romans 4:2, Paul basically says that if Abraham had been made righteous by his works, he would have been able to glory in himself, but not in God. But when Abraham believed God, trusted that God would do what He said, he gave God glory.

People do all kinds of things in the name of religion to try to glorify or please God. They go on pilgrimages, they flagellate themselves, they bathe in "holy" rivers, they abase themselves. But none of those things bring glory to God; they only draw attention to the ones who are doing them. There is only one way to bring glory to God: Believe Him! Take Him at His word. That is what Abraham discovered, and what I trust you have discovered, as well.

Have you ever known people you couldn't believe? It cuts right to the core of their character, doesn't it? Being able to believe someone, and acting on that belief, shows ultimate respect and honor for that person. Scripture says that "he that believeth not God hath made him a liar" (1 John 5:10). Believing God brings glory to God. Not believing Him dishonors Him.

This is at the heart of what it means to have faith. Seeing first, and then believing, is not faith. If Abraham had waited nine months for Isaac to be born, another nine months for Jacob, and so on until there were a few hundred descendants running around, and then said, "Okay, God, I believe You"—what kind of faith would that have been? Faith is evidence of a righteous heart. If my eye is healthy, I will see. If my ear is healthy, I will hear. If my heart is healthy, I will believe. And God will get the glory.

Salvation By Grace Receives God's Gift

Salvation by grace receives God's gift—but in a special way. Look at Romans 4:3: "It was counted unto him for righteousness." The same Greek word translated "counted" in verse 3 is translated "imputed" and "reckoned" in the same chapter:

- Verse 3: "it was counted unto him"
- Verse 6: "God imputeth righteousness"
- Verse 8: "the Lord will not impute sin"
- Verse 9: "that faith was reckoned"
- Verse 10: "how was it then reckoned
- Verse 11: "might be imputed"
- Verse 22: "therefore it was imputed"
- Verse 23: "that it was imputed to him"
- Verse 24: "us also, to whom it shall he imputed"

Over and over and over again, Paul is talking about something called imputation or reckoning. Anything mentioned this many times in a single chapter of Scripture must be important. It is not only important—It is the very heart of our salvation! Righteousness was imputed to us, just as it was imputed to Abraham.

When my wife and I send extra money to our son who is an overseas missionary, we do it in a very simple way. We simply deposit the money in his checking account here in the United States, and he accesses it in his country. He doesn't do anything except believe that we sent the money, and then receive it. He is free to withdraw it and benefit from it. That is imputation. It simply means that something has been credited to the account of another.

Romans 4:25 says Christ was delivered up to crucifixion for our offenses, not His. Paul explains it further in 2 Corinthians 5:21 by saying, "For he [God] hath made him to be sin for us, who knew no sin." That is a perfect description of imputation. One moment Jesus had no sin, the next moment He had our sin. One moment my son's bank account did not have extra funds in it, the next moment it did. Imputation is a transaction, a declaration, that must simply be believed in order to be received.

It was by imputation that you became a sinner before you were born. Adam's sin was imputed to you (charged to your account) because of your being one of his descendants. The sin of the entire human race was imputed to Jesus Christ (transferred to His account) because He is our Savior. And His righteousness, as the last Adam (1 Corinthians 15:45), was imputed to us (credited to our account) to make us righteous before God.

The Old Testament prefigurement of this transaction is found in Leviticus 16:21-22. The high priest would lay his hands on the head of the scapegoat and figuratively transfer the sins of the people onto the goat. The goat would then be sent out into the wilderness, never to return, as a picture of the sins of the people being carried away.

How do you receive the righteousness of Christ? By grace through faith. By believing that His righteousness has been credited to your account before God.

The Grace David Described

Not only does Paul tell us of the grace that Abraham discovered, but also of the grace that David described out of his own experience. In Romans 4:6-8, we read that "David also describeth the blessedness of the man, unto whom God imputeth righteousness without works ... Blessed is the man to whom the Lord will not impute sin."

How is it that David could personally describe this grace, this non-imputation of sin to his account? We know of David's terrible sin with Bathsheba and Uriah the Hittite as recounted in 2 Samuel 11. Adultery, murder, lying, and coverup—David's failure was a black episode in the life of the man after God's own heart. David tells in Psalm 32 of the horrors of hiding his sin and the blessedness of confessing it (see Romans 4). David was guilty of sin and deserved to die, but by God's grace David's sin was not charged to his account. The Old Testament sacrifices of bulls and goats temporarily covered his sin, and ultimately the sinless Lamb of God, Jesus Christ, paid for David's sin. David received forgiveness and righteousness instead of death. All by grace.

Perhaps you have been through a tragic time of sin and come to realize the grace and forgiveness provided for you through the death of Christ. If so, you, like David, could write a description of the blessedness of not having your sin charged to your account, and His righteousness credited to your account. Let's see how David describes, the righteousness that comes by grace through faith.

Iniquities Forgiven

"Blessed are they whose iniquities are forgiven" (Romans 4:7). In order for God to forgive your iniquity, God has to pay the price. There are no free pardons in heaven or anywhere else. If any sin is forgiven, the one who does the forgiving is the one who bears the penalty.

Let's suppose that my friend steals ten dollars from me and comes later stricken with guilt and confesses his sin. I forgive him, and we go on our way. But it cost me ten dollars to forgive him, didn't it? Somebody pays whenever there is forgiveness. That price to be paid is what put Jesus Christ on the cross. God didn't overlook sin when He forgave us. He acknowledged it and said, "Somebody has to pay." Amazing grace allowed Jesus to pay what we owed in order that we could be forgiven.

Sins Are Covered

Again in verse 7, we see that "sins are covered." Here's something that God does with our sin that I could never do with my friend's sin of stealing my money. God covers it so that it is never seen or remembered again. Micah 7:19 says God casts all our sins into the depths of the sea. Isaiah 38:17 says God has cast our sins behind His back. Psalm 103:12 says as far as the east is from the west, God has removed our sins from us.

When I forgive my friend, I think of his sin every time I see him. When God forgives us, our sins are gone, never to be seen or remembered again.

Sin Is Not Imputed

Romans 4:8 gives us our final descriptive from David: "Blessed is the man to whom the Lord will not impute sin." That's it. When Christ takes your sins, you will never have them imputed, charged, reckoned, or counted to your account again. He gets your sins, you get His righteousness.

The Grace Paul Discloses

Through a tradition-shaking disclosure, Paul finally clarifies the mystery, if you will, about grace.

First, this grace is for everyone, Jews and Gentiles alike. He has recorded Abraham's discovery and David's description of this gift from God. But are they the only ones who can receive this grace? Romans 4:12 says that grace is for all who walk in Abraham's steps of faith, whether of the circumcision (the Jews) or not (the Gentiles).

Secondly, Paul discloses that Abraham was counted as righteous by God solely on the basis of faith, not on the basis of any ritual, such as circumcision. Granted, circumcision was a sign, and a seal, of the covenant established between God and Abraham (verse 11). But verse 10 holds the key, where Paul asks the critical question: Was Abraham counted as righteous by God before he was circumcised or after? He was counted righteous "not in circumcision, but in uncircumcision" (verse 10). In fact, circumcision came as a seal of the righteousness he had already attained with God (verse 11).

The application for us today is that no ritual, human effort, ordinance, exercise, or qualification will make it possible for us to be made righteous by God. No nothing! The only way to receive His righteousness is the way Abraham, David, and Paul did—by faith, "if we believe on him that raised up Jesus our Lord from the dead" (Romans 4:24). When we agree with God about our sin, and believe His promise to take it away in Christ, it is taken away, and we, in return, are credited with the righteousness, of Christ!

Have you received the grace of God by faith? Could you describe it by personal experience? Can you share its simple truth with another? If not, receive it today.

Application

1. Chart the following events in Abraham's life, writing a brief description of what happened at each point:

    - Genesis 12:1, 4 God told him to Get out his country and leave his relatives and father's house and goto land God

    - Genesis 12:2; 13:16 had for him the went will He would become a great nation + God would bless him passed thru Sichem

    - Genesis 15:2-3 He questioned God about having an heir or son

    - Genesis 15:5 His descendants would be as vast as the stars

    - Genesis 15:6 He believed in the Lord + counted it as righteousness

    - Genesis 15:18 With abraham, the Lord made a covenant His seed would get land from river of Egypt unto river Euphrates

    - Genesis 17:1-9 He made a covenant, make him a great nation and inherit all of Canaan

    - Genesis 17:10-11 It has would come from his seed, changed his name to Abraham Every child would be circumcised and would be a token of the covenant

Now, answer the question which Paul raises in Romans 4:10: "How was it [Abraham's righteousness] then reckoned? when he was in circumcision, or in uncircumcision?

In uncircumcision

Why is Abraham called the "father of all them that believe" (Romans 4:11)? *because he believed and was made righteous by faith*

Babies learn to walk by following in their father's footsteps. What does this analogy mean in Romans 4:12 in relationship to our faith? *We follow abraham's faith by walking by faith*

2. How does Romans 4:16b-17b relate to Ephesians 2:11-12, 16, 18-19 (remember: Ephesians was written to a predominantly Gentile audience)? *We come to salvation by faith in the blood of Jesus*

How do these passages relate to Romans 11:13, 17, 20?

We are saved by grace faith comes by hearing the word

What can you conclude about the faith relationship, that began with Abraham? To whom has it now been extended?

You have to have a faith to be saved this includes all of creation

By what other means can man find a right standing with God? *No other means*

How does 1 Timothy 2:5-6 support what is presented in the above passages of Scripture?

There is only one mediator and God through whom we are saved Jesus the Christ

3. Fill in the following blanks based on what you have learned about righteousness by faith:

"When I placed my _faith_ in Jesus Christ, God transferred my _unrightness_ to Christ and transferred His _righteousness_ to me. The only thing I did to set this transaction in motion was the same thing Abraham did: I _believed_ God" (Genesis 15:6).

4. Find the word in 1 Corinthians 6:20 and 7:23 that is a familiar one in today's commercial shopping environment.

bought _price_

What was the "price" that Paul refers to? _Jesus death on the cross by his blood_

Who paid it? _Jesus Christ_

What was purchased? *our salvation redemption*

Who received what was purchased? *we did*

Describe an experience in your life where you forgave someone for something. What price did you have to pay in order to forgive them? *my pride*

In light of Christ having paid a price for your forgiveness, what does that make you (Romans 1:14)? *a debtor*

Digging Deeper

To gain a practical sense of David's experience in Psalm 32:1-2, do the following exercise. Use a spare checkbook register to keep a "Righteousness Register" for a couple of weeks. Begin with "Righteousness" in the balance column (at peace with God; Romans 5:1; 8:1). If you sin, write in what you did, write "Sin" in the debit column, and "Unrighteousness" in the balance column. When you confess your sin, enter "Imputation" in the credit column and "Righteousness" in the balance column. Continue this for a couple of weeks to gain perspective on the meaning of God's crediting righteousness to your account through Christ.

HOW TO BE STRONG IN THE FAITH

Overview

You'll need the same two things Abraham had in order to have strong faith: a great problem and a greater God. If you respond like Abraham did, you'll have strong faith, too.

Introduction: Romans 4:16-25

In our last lesson, we saw how two heroes of the faith, Abraham and David, enjoyed the blessings of imputation. Abraham had righteousness imputed to him (Genesis 15:6) on the basis of his faith, and David did not have his sin imputed to him (charged to his account, Psalm 32:2) on the basis of his belief that God would forgive him. Faith results in righteousness and cleansing from sin. It is the pivotal element in the Christian life. We live by faith.

Imagine two letters that have been placed in the mailbox. One letter is on crisp, embossed, very expensive stationery. It is typed impeccably. It is full of cogent thoughts, not one word is misspelled, and it has not a smudge on it. But it is placed in the mailbox with no stamp. Another letter, written in pencil, on inferior paper, with many misspellings, smudged and dirty, is dropped into the same mailbox, but this letter has a stamp. Which letter is going to be delivered? The one that is beautiful with no stamp, or the one that, though inferior, has a stamp on it? Since all of us have had the experience of dropping something in the mail without a stamp, you know the answer. In the Christian life, faith is the stamp.

Now some of us may look better than others, dress better than others, speak better than others. But do you know what God looks for? God looks for the stamp of faith upon our lives. Looking, dressing, and speaking well are all fine. I am not suggesting that those things are incompatible with faith. But I am saying that those things without faith will get you nowhere in the Christian life.

In this lesson, we will talk about how to have faith, but not just any faith—a strong faith. The challenges of living in our modern world require strong faith. And I believe that with every day that passes, the need for a stronger faith grows.

When God called Abraham in Genesis 12, He told him that all the nations of the world were going to be blessed through him. God did not intend for the Jewish nation to be simply a reservoir of blessing. He wanted to make them a channel of blessing, that through them all the nations of the world would be blessed. And God wants to do the same through you as a spiritual descendant of Abraham. But to be a channel of blessing, you will have to have strong faith.

Discussion

Our key passage for discovering how to have strong faith is Romans 4:16-25. This passage, as we discovered in our last lesson, reveals how Abraham discovered that faith was the key to righteousness with God. And in verse 20, we find our key verse for growing strong in faith: "He (Abraham) staggered not at the promise of God through unbelief; but was strong in faith, giving glory to God." Isn't that a great statement? Abraham did not stagger in unbelief at the promises God was making to him, but exercised strong faith! Then, in verses 23 and 24 we discover that "it was not written for his (Abraham's) sake alone ... But for us also." God wants us to exercise the same strong faith that Abraham did. It is clear that what happened to Abraham long ago is an example and a lesson for us today.

Now why is faith important? The answer is so simple: Because you cannot please God without it! Hebrews 11:6 says it as plainly as possible: "But without faith it is impossible to please him." If you please God, it doesn't matter whom you displease. And if you displease God, it doesn't really matter whom you please. And the way to please God is to believe Him.

Not only is it impossible to please God without faith, but it is impossible to be saved without faith: "For by grace are ye saved through faith" (Ephesians 2:8), and "therefore being justified by faith, we have peace with God through our Lord Jesus Christ" (Romans 5:1)—these verses say it well. Anyone reading these pages can be saved if they, will put their faith where God put their sins, upon the Lord Jesus Christ.

The difference between people who are saved and those who are not is faith. And the difference between those who overcome in this life and have victory, and those who don't, is strong faith. Abraham wasn't perfect, but he was victorious, because he had strong faith. And that is the kind of faith God wants you to have today.

First, let me say what faith is not. Faith is not a hunch or positive thinking. Faith is not believing everything will work out. Faith is not responding to emotions, feelings, icicles up and down your spine, or miracles and signs. Faith is not believing simply that God can; faith is knowing that God will. True faith is taking God at His word. Strong faith is deaf to doubt, dumb to discouragement, and blind to impossibilities. It *knows* that God will. Now this is the kind of faith we need.

Strong Faith Is Received As a Gift of God

First of all, strong faith is received as a gift of God. Look at Romans 4:16: "Therefore it is of faith, that it might be by grace."

Now, what is grace? Grace is the unmerited favor that God gives to sinners such as we, where there is no merit whatsoever. Salvation is the grace-gift of God. You don't generate faith; you are totally depraved by nature and there is nothing in you that can generate faith. As a matter of fact, the Bible says in Ephesians 2:1, "And you hath he quickened, who were dead in trespasses and sins." It's not just that we are sick with sin. We are dead in sin! So, grace is not a reward for our faith. Our faith is the gift of God's grace.

But once we have received the gift of faith it must be exercised. Like Abraham, we must exercise faith and believe (grasp, walk in, depend on, trust in) the statements God makes to us. God gives us faith, but He does not exercise faith for us.

Think of it this way: God gives you lungs and oxygen, but does not breathe for you. God gives you eyes and light waves, but does not see for you. You can choose to shut down those wonderful gifts at any time. Anyone who says they cannot believe has not heard God speak, because faith is nothing more than a response to the promises of God. Faith has to have an object, and Abraham's object was God and His promises (see Romans 4:13-16 and the references to "the promise").

The Bible says in Romans 10:17, "Faith cometh by hearing, and hearing by the word of God." Dwight L. Moody was the Billy Graham of his day, the greatest American evangelist of the late 19th century. Moody said he used to close his Bible and pray for faith but his faith never would grow. And then he said he read Romans 10:17. And he said he stopped praying for faith and started reading his Bible and faith just burst into flames in his heart!

Do you want to develop strong faith? Then find the strongest promises of God and believe them! The stronger the promise, the stronger the faith.

Strong Faith Releases the Grace of God

Faith is received as a gift of God and then it releases the grace of God. Look in Romans 4:16 again: "Therefore it is of faith, that it might be by grace; to the end the promise might be sure." Faith links us to grace. We're not ultimately saved by faith. We're saved by grace, but it is faith that links us to grace.

It is true that Jesus died on the cross and paid for your sins, but that does you absolutely no good until you put your faith in Him. Matthew 13:58 records the time when Jesus was in His hometown of Nazareth and could do few mighty works because the people had no faith. Faith unlocks the benefits of the grace of God.

The stronger our faith gets, the more we realize the grace of God, as did Abraham (Romans 4:16). The only way we can be sure that our faith will be effective is to trust totally in the grace of God. Do I know I am saved? Absolutely! But is it because I have a lot of self-confidence that I can say that? No! It is because I have NO self-confidence (as far as salvation goes) that I can say that. My only confidence regarding salvation is confidence in the grace of God and what Jesus did on the cross for me. And it is my faith which keeps grace alive in my heart.

The story is told of the great cheer that went up outside the gates of heaven when the word started circulating among the believers waiting to be admitted that prayer meeting attendance was not being counted. Well, if any of our "good" deeds are counted, we are in trouble. Why? Because our good deeds will not buy a ticket to heaven. We have all sinned and come short in some way or another. The only thing that has not fallen short is the grace of God, which substitutes for all of our shortcomings.

So, what does strong faith do? It releases the grace of God in us that we might enjoy the free gift of salvation.

Strong Faith Respects the Greatness of God

In Romans 4:17 we find two things that only God could do, and Abraham believed them both: God can bring life from death, and can make something out of nothing. God is a great God, and strong faith shows respect for that greatness by believing what greatness can accomplish.

Remember that Abraham was one hundred years old when God spoke to him, and his wife was ninety years old—a little past the normal age for having children! But Abraham believed that God could produce millions of descendants when there was not yet one child to come from Sarah and him.

Our God is a great God! If your faith is weak, get to know God better. Glance at your problem, gaze at your God. Imitate

Abraham, who "against hope believed in hope" (verse 18). There are no hopeless situations with God. If you think your situation is impossible, think about Abraham's. He and his wife, ready for their wheelchairs, are told to begin a new nation! But Abraham decided to hope, and put faith in God. If God came through for Abraham, He will come through for you.

Strong Faith Regards the Guidance of God

Verses 20 and 21 reveal Abraham's response to the guidance of God for his and Sarah's future: "He staggered not at the promise of God through unbelief; but was strong in faith, giving glory to God; and being fully persuaded that, what he had promised, he was able also to perform." Now the point is this: Who took the steps here to insure that Isaac, the son of promise, would be born?

This was not an immaculate conception. Abraham and Sarah entered into normal relations and the blessing of God produced their son. Strong faith regards the guidance of God and responds with action. This was characteristic of Abraham, as Hebrews 11:8 tells us: "By faith Abraham, when he was called ... obeyed."

The book of James discusses Abraham's faith in a different but complementary light (James 2:21-23). James says that Abraham was justified by works when he offered Isaac on the attar in obedience to God (Genesis 22:1-13). This was after he had already been declared justified by faith in Genesis 15:6. So what is James trying to say? Simply this: Abraham's actions of faith provided proof of his faith. We are not saved by works, but we are saved by a faith that works. We are justified before God by faith alone, but that faith is never alone. It is always accompanied by the works of faith.

James and Paul are not in contradiction regarding Abraham. They are both absolutely accurate. Abraham was justified by faith when he believed God, and he was justified by works when he demonstrated his faith in obedience. Faith responds to the guidance of God. Faith is acting upon what we know to be true. We faithfully obey. And I'm going to tell you something. If you have Abraham's faith (belief) as described by Paul, you'll have Abraham's faith (works) as described by James. They go together where there is strong faith.

Strong Faith Reflects the Glory of God

Look again in verse 20: "He [Abraham] staggered not at the promise of God through unbelief; but was strong in faith, giving glory to God." Would you like to give glory to God? The stronger your faith, the more radiant His glory. Do you know what is the greatest thing you could do to give God glory? It is not to give a million dollars to missions. Or to give your body as a martyr. It is not to go overseas as a missionary. The greatest thing you can do to glorify God is to say, "God, You are trustworthy and I believe You." Abraham "was strong in faith, giving glory to God."

Think about your own children. What blesses the heart of a parent the most? Gifts? A clean room? Good grades? No, it is simple, childlike faith. Faith in protection and faith in provision. Don't parade about your belief in a good God, a strong God, and all the rest of it, and then fail to believe Him.

How strong is your faith today? Have you received faith as a gift of God? Do that first. Then connect with His grace, greatness, guidance, and glory—all by strong faith!

Application

1. Read Genesis 12:10-20. What part of Abraham's faith grew weak? *He didn't believe God could protect him.*

    From your reading of Genesis 11-12, and given Abraham's age when he came to know God, approximately how mature was Abraham's faith at this point? *not that mature*

What does this show you about the nature of strong faith?

You don't doubt and fear

Given that God continued to use Abraham, what does his Word say about the life of faith?

You have to believe and not doubt You believe God will fulfill his promises

2. Read Hebrews 11:8-12. How much specific direction did Abraham have when he first obeyed God (verse 8)?

he didn't know where he was going but trusted God to guide him

The word "strange" is used to describe the country where Abraham sojourned (verse 9). What must have seemed strange about this country?

He didn't know the area or the people.

Describe a time in your life when you acted in obedience to God, but when your "sojourn" seemed strange.

Paid IRS penalty

Describe the degree of understanding which you ultimately had about the purposes of God. *not totally Understanding*

3. Read Romans 10:17. If faith comes by hearing the Word of God, list some areas in your life where God's Word is increasing your faith:

The Situation   The Word of God

a. *finances*   *my God shall supply all my needs according to riches in glory*

b.

c.

4. God promised to bring "something out of nothing" for Abraham and Sarah. Have you seen God do the same in your life (finances, character trait, vocation)?

Yes,

What happens to strong faith when the promise is not forthcoming? *It is tested*

5. Regarding "faith" and "works" as discussed in James 2, list an area of your life where works would give greater evidence of your faith.

Why are these works not more evident? What is holding you back?

Digging Deeper

Is faith a verb or a noun? Your dictionary will list it as a noun, but it is one of those words that could easily be used as a verb (e.g., "I'm going to have to faith my way through this situation"). We speak of faith as an action, a verb, because faith needs to demonstrate its existence. If you say, "I have faith," someone else can say, "Prove it." It's like Paul saying in 1 Corinthians 13 that "love is ..." and then listing a number of proofs of the existence of true love. Start a list on a card that you can keep handy over the next 7 days. Title the card, "Faith is." See how many practical evidences of faith in your life you can list. It's a way to prove to yourself that, indeed, you have faith!

HOW TO HAVE A ROCK-SOLID FAITH

Overview

*Between conversion and Christlikeness stands conflict. Some new
believers get discouraged before understanding that pressure is
part of the plan. Paul's explanation of the process gives hope for
the future.*

Introduction: Romans 5:1-5

We are deep into the good news of the Gospel in
Romans. We heard the bad news in Romans 1-3, that
we have all sinned in God's sight. Then we spent two lessons
in Romans 4 where Paul uses Abraham's faith to explain the
kind of faith we should have. We've talked about faith and
strong faith, and now we will talk about rock-solid faith— faith
that will not be moved regardless of what comes against it.

Every believer must learn how to put spiritual steel and concrete in his life to withstand the tests that will come. Some tests will be specifically directed at his faith; other tests will be just the tests of life which will require strong faith. Either way, without rock-solid faith, the believer will be tossed about like a chip of bark in a raging stream. Many Christians today are being swept away in floods of affliction. They don't have an anchor that will hold in the storm. On the contrary, their life seems to be built on eggshells and jello. They are weak and floundering saints. God wants us to be strong and not give up. He wants us to look up and stand fast, trusting in His foundation that is sure.

As the Constitution is for the United States, so the book of Romans is a foundation for the Christian's faith. Would you like to have rock-solid faith in the midst of storms? Then this lesson from the book of Romans will help you to develop that kind of faith.

When God gives you salvation, He's only beginning with you. The Bible says in Philippians 1:6, "he which hath begun a good work in you will perform it until the day of Jesus Christ." So getting saved does not mean we are finished. We're only beginning His building process in us. And the building must have a rock-solid foundation.

Discussion

In Romans 5:1-4, we are going to discover four steps by which God develops rock-solid faith in believers:

Therefore being justified by faith, we have peace with God through our Lord Jesus Christ: by whom also we have access by faith into this grace wherein we stand, and rejoice in hope of the glory of God. And not only so, but we glory in tribulations also: knowing that tribulation worketh patience; and patience, experience; and experience, hope: and hope maketh not ashamed; because the love of God is shed abroad in our hearts by the Holy Ghost which is given unto us.

Here's a question that may be a little tricky: When God saves you, does He give you peace or does He give you tribulation? The answer is, "Yes!" He gives you both. We read about the peace of God in verse 1 and the tribulation in verse 3. Don't think, dear friend, that when you get saved, that all you get is peace. There will be heartache, tears, disappointment—in short, there will be tribulation. He will teach you how to have peace through the tribulation, but He will not spare you the suffering.

Here is how He does it:

Conversion Brings Conflict

First of all, we need to recognize that conversion is going to bring conflict—perhaps more conflict than before you were converted.

The word "tribulation" in verse 3 means pressure. The word was used to describe the crushing of grapes to make wine or crushing olives to get oil. God wants to build into your character the wine and the oil of His strength and His love. Just as a diamond starts as a lump of coal that's been under pressure for a long, long time, so God begins to build value into us by using pressure.

But it is not random, capricious, or arbitrary pressure. It is purposeful, and He is over it all, watching carefully that you are not pressured beyond what you are able to bear (1 Corinthians 10:13). You must understand that God is over all and when you come to Jesus, you're going to come into conflict and pressure. Pressure, leading to conflict, can come from one of four sources.

Pressure Comes From the World

The Bible says in Romans 12:2, "be not conformed to this world. The minute you come to Jesus, this world begins trying to squeeze you into its mold—in business, in education, in entertainment, in politics, in every area of life. There will be incredible pressure upon the child of God to reject the thinking of the kingdom of God and stay with the way you thought as a non-Christian. That's why Paul says in Romans 12:2 that you must renew your mind.

Pressure Comes From the Flesh

Once you are saved, your new nature comes into conflict with your old Adamic nature. The proclivity to sin is still there. You feel it. I feel it. You never get beyond it. The Bible calls it "the flesh." It is an enemy inside the fort of your faith. You're going to feel a civil war within you. I felt it when I first got saved as a teenage boy. I can remember a particular time after I had given my heart to Jesus, I was out with some friends and an incredible temptation came to me. And I can remember the war that was going on. My flesh said, "Adrian, that's something you want to do. That's something you need to do. Everybody else is doing it." And the Holy Spirit was saying to me, "No, you're different. You cannot do that." I felt the biggest battle going on in my heart as I prayed and struggled as a new Christian. Galatians 5:17 confirms our experience: "the flesh lusteth against the Spirit, and the Spirit against the flesh: and these are contrary the one to the other."

Pressure Comes From the Devil

We never really understand the power of Satan until we get saved. When a Christian says, "Well, I don't have any difficulty with the devil," I know that the believer and the devil are probably traveling in the same direction. If the believer will turn around, he'll have a collision with the devil instead of being in collusion with him. When you give your heart to Jesus, Satan is going to level all of the artillery of hell against you.

Pressure Comes from God

Finally, there is a different source of pressure. While the world, the flesh, and the devil bring pressure to slow the believer down, God brings pressure to grow the believer up. The Bible says, "for whom the Lord loveth he chasteneth, and scourgeth every son whom he receiveth" (Hebrews 12:6). You see, God is not trying to make you happy. God wants to make you holy. Temptation, testing, and trials are a part of life. It's a false gospel that says if you come to Christ there will be no adversity, misfortune, persecution, or pain. God will allow pressure, or send it, to develop the character of Christ in us. As muscle grows when it pushes against the barbell, so the faith of the believer grows as it overcomes the pressures of the world, the flesh, the devil, and a loving Father.

Conflict Teaches Constancy

What happens when the believer learns to withstand and overcome pressure over time? Constancy develops. Steadfastness results. Consistency in faith arises. Notice again that "tribulation worketh patience" (Romans 5:3). The word "patience" means constancy, the quality of being steadfast and unmovable. Constancy means rock-solid faith. As Paul says in 1 Corinthians 15:58, faith that is "stedfast, unmoveable, always abounding in the work of the Lord."

In reality, when the pressure comes, it doesn't make you; it just reveals what you're made of. The same sun that melts the ice, hardens the clay. If I asked whether you want to be steadfast and victorious in faith, you would probably say, "Yes." If I asked whether you want to have tribulation, you would likely say, "No." But having the one is getting the other. Tribulation brings steadfastness. Conflict teaches constancy.

Not everyone welcomes conflict and pressure when they come. People usually react in one of four ways when conflict appears, regardless of the source:

You Can Retreat From Conflict

Some people just run away from conflict. They wither physically or emotionally, they get a plane ticket, take a pill, turn up a bottle, use a needle, or take a gun. One man said, "The way to fight a woman is with your hat." They said, "What do you mean?" He said, "Grab it and run." Instead of facing the conflict—and solving and growing from the pressure— they run. This reaction never produces constancy.

You Can Resent Conflict

While some flee, others will stay, giving a good impression on the outside. But in truth, they deeply resent the conflict when it comes. They reason this way: "I gave my heart to Jesus Christ. I went down the aisle, I got baptized, I started going to Sunday School, I started tithing, and now look what has happened to me." They pout, get mad at God, and become cynical about the Christian life. As a result, the conflict never has the intended positive result.

You Can Resign Yourself to Conflict

Others resign, cave in, and give up. They lie down on the field, surrender their shield, and give in to discouragement and despondency. They develop a martyr complex and think that every conflict that comes their way is their cross to bear. Their spiritual gift becomes "suffering," and they spend the rest of their Christian life requesting prayer for the crisis du jour.

Obviously, none of these three strategies are God's plan for the believer. Tribulation is sent to work patience, conflict to work constancy. So how do we allow trials to have their perfect result (James 1:4)?

You Can Resolve to Follow Him

Resolve by faith that you will follow Jesus Christ, come what may. Faith is shown more in patience and constancy than in any other way. If your faith stays true when trouble comes, you will endure. Faith is not receiving the things you want nearly so much as it is accepting from God the things He gives. Faith is the power to do what you ought (stand firm in tests), not a license to do what you feel (retreat, resent, or resign). Tribulation works patience. Don't try to wiggle out of what God is allowing. Job said, "Though he slay me, yet will I trust in him" (Job 13:15).

Constancy Develops Character

While the King James Version translates Romans 5:4 as "And patience, [worketh] experience," a more precise translation is that patience works character. Constancy, or steadfastness, over time develops into character—the characteristic of rock-solid faith.

God is going to allow you to go through the fire of affliction to test you. Why? Because the faith that can't be tested can't be trusted. As the fire of testing refines your character, the dross comes to the top and can be eliminated. That's the way God builds character.

The times that I've grown the most, and the times you will grow the most, are the times when things are the hardest. While we might think God would give us a relaxed, comfortable environment in which to grow rock-solid faith, exactly the opposite is true. Hebrews 5:8 says, "Though he [Christ] were a Son, yet learned he obedience by the things which he suffered." If Jesus, from a human perspective, learned obedient faith through sufferings, we can expect to learn it the same way.

While "experience" is perhaps not the first choice for the translation in verse 4, experience is still a critical element of the character-building process. A successful business man was asked by his protégé how to become successful. "Good decisions," replied the veteran. "I see," said the younger. "And how do you learn to make good decisions?" "Experience," answered the older. Risking one more question, the young man continued, "And how do you get experience?" "Bad decisions," ended the wise one.

God will allow you to make bad decisions for three reasons: so that you have the experience of suffering, so that you can try again and make a better decision and succeed, and to show you that constancy is what builds character.

Conversion brings conflict. Conflict teaches constancy. Constancy develops character. If you will stay in the fire, God knows what He is doing. Most of us just want to get out of the lire. But they say that the person who is refining the gold knows it's pure when he can see his face reflected in it. What God is looking for is His character, His likeness, reflected in our lives.

Character Will Give Confidence

The last part of God's plan for building rock-solid faith is to build confidence manifested through hope. Romans 5:4 says, "and experience, [worketh] hope." What does the Bible mean by "hope"? It doesn't mean "maybe so" or "it might be." No, when the Bible uses the word "hope" it means rock-solid faith. For example, the second coming of Jesus is called the blessed hope (Titus 2:13). That doesn't mean the blessed maybe. Do we think Jesus "might" return? No, our blessed hope is that we know He is going to return. Hebrews 6:19 calls our salvation a hope that is like an anchor, rock- solid: "Which hope we have as an anchor of the soul, both sure and steadfast."

You say, "I want a rock-solid faith." What you're really saying is, I want conversion which brings conflict, and conflict that teaches constancy, and constancy that develops character, and character that gives confidence. That's what you get if you ask for rock-solid faith.

And hope is the essence of confidence. Hope is faith in the future tense. It believes God as much for what it cannot see in the future as for what it can see in the present. The believer becomes like God in a sense—not bound or constrained by time. Future faith is as real as present-tense faith. But the future faith is called hope. "And hope maketh not ashamed ...(Romans 5:5). That means it never disappoints.

I trust you are confident about the future. If you are not, it may be because you don't yet have the faith I am talking about. You can go from pressure to perseverance, from conflict to Christlikeness, by beginning a faith relationship with Christ today. Won't you consider doing that if you haven't already? And if you have—then welcome to the future, where hope never disappoints!

Application

1. Read 1 Peter 4:12-13. What words does Peter use to describe what his readers were going through? *fiery*

   trials

What reaction were they apparently having?

they didn't understand the trials

Instead of surprise, what should be their reaction (verse 13)?

they should rejoice

What does the phrase "partakers of Christ's sufferings" (verse 13) mean?

We will suffer as Christ did, persecution crucified with Christ

2. Read Galatians 3:1-3. What can happen to a Christian who is walking in the Spirit (verse 3)?

they can turn back to old lifestyle and backslide

According to Galatians 5:17, what kind of war is being waged in the heart of every believer? *the flesh wars against the spirit so you can't do what you should do*

What is required if one is not to yield to the pressures of the flesh (Galatians 5:16)? *you have to walk in the spirit*

Paul lists a number of areas from which fleshly pressures might arise. Based on your own evaluation of his list, group them under the following categories (Galatians 5:19-21):

- Spiritual: *Idolatry heresies Uncleaness*

- Sexual: *adultery fornication*

- Relational: *envyings*

- Personal behavior: *drunkeness wrath strife*

3. Read 2 Corinthians 2:11, Ephesians 6:11-12, Luke 22:31, and 1 Peter 5:8. In light of these passages, write a brief paragraph describing the devil's strategies to derail the believer's life. *He puts lies in your mind, He deceives causes division + strife*

4. Read Hebrews 5:8. How does Hebrews12:6 offer insight to this passage? *God suffered + we learn obedience through suffering*

How difficult do you think it might be for a person to learn the admonition to voluntarily die? *It's difficult to die to self.*

What does Luke 14:27 suggest that every believer must be prepared to do, either spiritually or perhaps even physically? *Every Christian needs to bear his own burden and die to self or even be martyred*

5. Learning to respond spiritually to the pressures of the spiritual life is a process. List areas of conflicts in your life under the heading of how you are currently responding to them (review the four responses from the lesson, if needed):

- Retreat / flee *I don't run away from the problem*

- Resent it *I have to confess any resentment*

- React passively / with resignation *I do spiritual warfare*

- Resolve to follow Christ *I try to follow Christ.*

Digging Deeper

Hebrews 12:3-13 is perhaps the most thorough presentation of how God allows pressures and conflicts to come into the lives of His children. In order to understand God's role as your Heavenly Father—personally allowing pressure and conflict to enter your life—complete the following exercise: Write out the entire passage (Hebrews 12:3-13) in paraphrase fashion, as a personal letter from God to you. Replace impersonal pronouns ("you") with your own name. Begin it with "Dear (your name)," and end it with "Your loving Heavenly Father." Keep it to read often—especially the next time you find yourself enduring spiritual pressure!

CPSIA information can be obtained
at www.ICGtesting.com
Printed in the USA
LVHW022214270319
612109LV00001B/1/P